THE MATERIAL OF CULTURE

THE MATERIAL OF CULTURE

RENAISSANCE MEDALS AND TEXTILES FROM THE ULRICH A. MIDDELDORF COLLECTION

PERRI LEE ROBERTS

GEORGIA MUSEUM *of* ART
UNIVERSITY *of* GEORGIA

October 26, 2013 – January 12, 2014

Published by the Georgia Museum of Art, University of Georgia.

Printed in China by Kings Time in an edition of 500.

Design: Nathan W. Moehlmann, Goosepen Studio & Press

Department of Publications: Hillary Brown and Mary Koon

Publications Interns: Noah Adler, Kate Douds,
Elizabeth Fontaine, Claire Ruhlin, Sarah Schatz

Library of Congress Cataloging-in-Publication Data

Roberts, Perri Lee.

The material of culture : Renaissance medals and textiles from the

Ulrich A. Middeldorf collection / Perri Lee Roberts. | pages cm

"Georgia Museum of Art, University of Georgia, October 26, 2013/January 12, 2014."

Includes bibliographical references.

ISBN 978-0-915977-82-6 – ISBN 0-915977-82-6

1. Medals, Renaissance–Exhibitions. 2. Textile fabrics, Renaissance–Exhibitions.

3. Middeldorf, Ulrich, 1901-1983–Art collections–Exhibitions. 4. Medals–Private

collections–Indiana–Bloomington–Exhibitions. 5. Textile fabrics–Private collections–

Indiana–Bloomington–Exhibitions. 6. Indiana University, Bloomington.

Art Museum–Exhibitions. I. Georgia Museum of Art. II. Title.

CJ6201.R63 2013 | 737'.22–dc23 | 2013029596

Partial support for the exhibitions and programs at the Georgia Museum
of Art is provided by the W. Newton Morris Charitable Foundation.
Individuals, foundations, and corporations provide additional support
through their gifts to the University of Georgia Foundation.

FRONT COVER ILLUSTRATION: *Giovanni Martino Hamerani (1646–1705), medal of Prince Livio Odesscalchi, 1689 (obverse).* IUAM, 87.26.2.95. BACK COVER ILLUSTRATION: *Italy, probably Tuscany, second half of the 15th century, orphrey band with Man of Sorrows, lampas, brocatelle.* IUAM, 91.143. FRONTISPIECE: *Italy, possibly Florence, late 15th century, silk and linen panel, cut velvet.* IUAM, 91.99.

CONTENTS

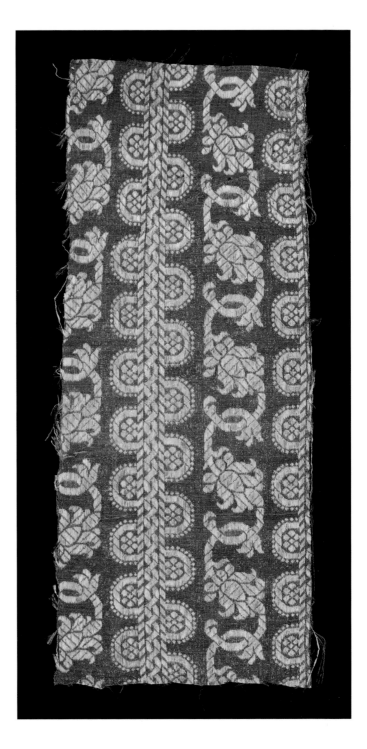

FOREWORD

Ulrich Middeldorf's stature as an art historian and scholar, professor and curator, advocate and administrator, is undisputed, although rarely recognized outside academia. As the man who reopened the Kunsthistorisches Institut of Florence in 1953 and directed its growth and influence for the next fifteen years, in the words of Perri Lee Roberts, he "established the 'Kunst' as the premier European research center for the study of art history."

This project celebrates another aspect of Middeldorf's life and career, that of the collector who saw in the object the underpinnings of connoisseurship. Art for Middeldorf, in its various forms, is a marker of culture, evidence of human achievement realized in concrete objects of beauty, of wonder, even of mystery. The cloth, medals, and plaquettes in this exhibition represent such art, artifacts of material culture that Middeldorf and his wife, Gloria, believed were essential to visual arts education.

Lynn Boland and Laura Valeri, along with our registrars, ably led by Tricia Miller, deserve acknowledgment for this project's realization, as do our editor Hillary Brown and the rest of the staff at the Georgia Museum of Art. We are also grateful to Adelheid M. Gealt and her staff at Indiana University Art Museum for their collaboration and their stewardship of the Middeldorf Collection.

Such a project as this one, viewed as of primarily "academic" interest, benefits greatly from the generosity and foresight of the Samuel H. Kress Foundation and the W. Newton Morris Charitable Foundation. We extend

OPPOSITE: *Italy, 17th century, textile fragment, silk and gilt metal strips.* IUAM, *87.26.1.668.*

sincere appreciation to Max Marmor and his board at the Kress Foundation and to Jack Sawyer and William Torres of the Morris Foundation.

The genesis of the project arose many years ago with Andrew Ladis's unstinting admiration for Ulrich and Gloria Middeldorf and through his great friendship with Bruce Cole and Heidi Gealt. He bequeathed the project to Perri Lee Roberts, his colleague and friend, who gave it her own interpretation. He would have been as grateful for her work as we are, and certainly as proud.

WILLIAM UNDERWOOD EILAND
Director

THE MATERIAL OF CULTURE

ULRICH ALEXANDER

MIDDELDORF:

SCHOLAR-COLLECTOR

The German-American art historian Ulrich Alexander Middeldorf (1901–1983; fig. 1) was a world-renowned scholar and connoisseur of fifteenth- and sixteenth-century Italian sculpture and drawings who published more than two hundred articles and books in the course of his long and prolific career.[1] Middeldorf was born in Strassfurt am Bode, Germany, and studied art history at the universities of Giessen, Munich, and Berlin with the distinguished scholars Heinrich Wölfflin, Adolf Goldschmidt, and August Liebmann Mayer. After receiving his doctorate in 1924 from Humboldt University of Berlin with a dissertation on late medieval German sculpture, he received a two-year fellowship from the Kunsthistorisches Institut (German Art Institute) in Florence. From 1926 to 1935, Middeldorf worked as the keeper of the photography collection at the Institut, building the collection and assisting Richard Offner with research on the monumental series the *Corpus of Florentine Painting*. During these years, he often traveled to London, where he became friendly with Sir George Hill, keeper of the department of coins and medals at the British Museum and, as of 1930, director of that institution; Hill also wrote *A Corpus of Italian Medals of the Renaissance Before Cellini*.[2] In response to the Nazis' rise to power, Middeldorf immigrated to the United States in 1935. Recommended by Bernard Berenson and sponsored by the wealthy Chicago businessman and art collector Max Epstein, he was appointed assistant professor in the art history department of the University of Chicago.

Over the course of the next eighteen years, Middeldorf became professor and chair of the art history department, director and president of the Renaissance Society at the University of Chicago, director and president of the College Art Association, chair of the Fifth Ward Art Center of Chicago, and honorary curator of sculpture at the Art Institute of Chicago. For Middeldorf, these were extremely busy years — besides his official posts, he published numerous articles and books on drawings, sculpture, medals, and plaquettes; organized exhibitions for the Renaissance Society and the Art Institute; recommended acquisitions of sculpture for the Art Institute; and taught and mentored graduate students.[3]

In 1953, Middeldorf returned to Florence to reopen the Kunsthistorisches Institut following its closure during World War II. As director, he greatly expanded its library holdings, facilities, programs, and collaborations with foreign scholars and foundations and thereby established the "Kunst" as the premier European research center for the study of art history. For his contributions to the arts, Middeldorf was recognized by the Italian government in 1962 with its highest honor, Commendatore Ordine al Merito della Repubblica Italiana. Following his retirement from the Kunsthistorisches Institut, in 1968, he served as the founding director of the newly established Istituto Roberto Longhi in Florence. In the final years of his career, Middeldorf continued to be an extremely active scholar, publishing, among other works, the catalogue *Sculptures from the Samuel H. Kress Collection: European Schools XIV–XIV* (1976) and *Renaissance Medals and Plaquettes* (1983). Ulrich Alexander Middeldorf died in his beloved Florence in February 1983.[4]

In his obituary of the scholar, Anthony Radcliffe, keeper emeritus of the Victoria and Albert Museum, London, emphasized the importance of the object for Middeldorf: "He was always insistent that art history should take as its starting-point the work of art itself.... A clear eye for quality, he [Middeldorf] believed was the most useful asset an art historian could acquire."[5] For Middeldorf, "art" was an inclusive term, encompassing the major, "fine" arts of painting, sculpture, and drawing as well as the equally important decorative or applied arts of ceramics, textiles, furniture, and metalwork. Early in his career, he acknowledged the significance of material culture to the study of art history in a review of a newly published catalogue of Medici porcelain: "Pottery and other products of the so-called minor arts introduce us intimately into the life of the past. They can evoke our forefathers in their most human aspects, while the major arts generally reveal them only in their most solemn elated moods. This explains the great charm and fascination with such a collection as that of the late Albert Figdoe [sic] for there the greatest love and understanding of its owner had brought together all the small, often insignificant looking remains of the past and had almost called them to life again in their interrelationship."[6]

Personal experience with artifacts of material culture was not only important for the scholar and connoisseur, but also, Middeldorf believed, in the education of art history students. Leading the discussion in a session titled "The Place of Connoisseurship in Art in Universities and Museums, with Particular Emphasis on the Minor Arts" at the College Art Association Conference in 1941, Professor Middeldorf stated his own point of view (as later reported): "He [Middeldorf] emphasized the importance of holding seminar discussions in the museum with the actual objects whenever possible. When, however, this was not feasible,

Gaspare Mola (ca. 1580–1640), medal of Grand Duke Ferdinand I de' Medici, 1608 (obverse). IUAM, 87.26.2.93.

even the study of shards of pottery would give the student the feeling of the quality of objects such as could never be obtained from a study of reproductions. He stressed also the importance of any sort of collecting with this in mind, that it was not necessary for objects to be of the first quality or even of considerable value, but that the very familiarity with things, which comes with collecting from an aesthetic point of view, is of inestimable value later when objects of greater importance and quality are examined."[7]

Middeldorf practiced what he preached. Following in the footsteps of Renaissance scholar collectors and nineteenth-century connoisseurs of the decorative arts, he collected in the areas of his scholarly expertise and interests, assembling 300 medals, 12 plaquettes, and more than 150 textile fragments from the fifteenth through the twentieth century. His widow, Gloria Middeldorf, gave these materials, together with hundreds of pieces of bobbin laces, twenty-seven works on paper, four paintings, and one bronze sculpture, to the Indiana University Art Museum (IUAM) in 1987 and 1991.

Bruce Cole, professor emeritus of art history at Indiana University and intimate friend of the couple, describes the Middeldorfs as inveterate collectors: "They didn't collect just to own. Rather they collected because they appreciated the individual aesthetic quality of the objects they bought, and because they were fascinated by the people and time that created them. . . . They bought what they liked, what they could afford, and what they loved."[8] Middeldorf never wrote about his own collecting habits, but some insight into his motivations as a collector may be gleaned from the few comments he made in passing. In the exhibition catalogue *Medals and Plaquettes from the Sigmund Morgenroth Collection* (1944), Middeldorf observes, "There is perhaps more sense in collecting medals and plaquettes than altar-pieces and monumental sculpture. While the latter were made for definite purposes, so that they lose a great deal of their meaning once they are torn from their original context, medals and plaquettes never, or rarely, had any other home than that of the collector."[9] A few years later, in a review of a new book on Italian plaquettes, he bemoans the fact that medals and plaquettes seem to have lost favor with collectors and scholars: "Plaquettes and medals are of the highest interest, artistically, iconographically, and in many other aspects. . . . Medals and plaquettes, indeed, are a wonderful material for the student of Renaissance art."[10]

In regard to his collection of textiles and bobbin laces — the majority of which are small remnants of much larger pieces — the published record is virtually silent.[11] Middeldorf wrote only two brief articles dealing with late medieval and Italian Renaissance textiles, late in his career;

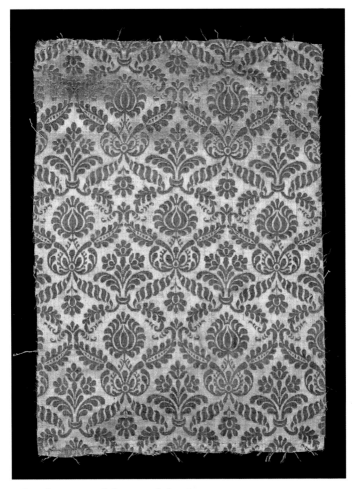

Italy, 16th century, textile fragment, silk damask. IUAM, *87.26.1.803.*

however, from correspondence preserved in the special collections of the Getty Research Institute Library, it is evident that he was fascinated with the history of textiles and, at the same time, frustrated by the paucity of scholarship in the field.[12] A letter from a woman who studied with him at the University of Chicago in the late 1940s confirms the fact that Middeldorf used his collections as

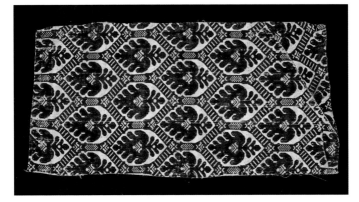

Italy or Spain, 16th–17th century, textile fragment, silk velvet. IUAM, *87.26.1.201.*

teaching tools. Thanking him for a copy of his recently
published article on the interrelationship of Florentine
textile patterns and contemporary sculpture, she writes,
"I was delighted to receive your *Pantheon* offprint, not
only for itself but because it reminded me of our Chicago
days and my first acquaintance with collecting and connoisseurship. I'll never forget those cupboards of yours
bulging with beautiful velvets and brocades."[13] In correspondence with Harold B. Burnham (1912–1973), curator of textiles at the Royal Ontario Museum of Canada,
Middeldorf described himself as "more collector than
student" of textiles of the fifteenth through seventeenth
centuries and expressed the hope that one day he would
to able to show Burnham his "collection of samples."[14]

The twenty-five medals, eight plaquettes, and thirty-
three textiles selected for this exhibition are, with few exceptions, Italian in origin and date from the mid-fifteenth
to the late seventeenth century. Most were made from
costly materials and were considered luxury items. The
wealthy consumers of medals, plaquettes, and silk textiles
were an elite segment of the population who considered

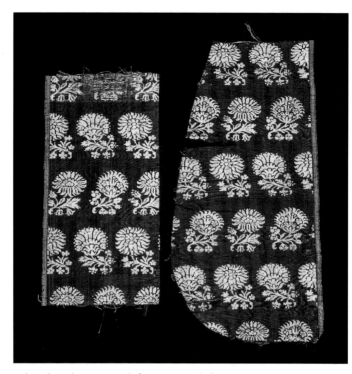

Italy, 16th–17th century, textile fragment, moired silk. IUAM, *87.26.1.340A.*

these items fashionable, displayable commodities and status symbols of social privilege. The works on display are typical examples of Italian Renaissance and Baroque decorative arts and represent the "little-seen objects" Middeldorf was keen to bring to the attention of his students and the general public to encourage appreciation and understanding of the material culture of a particularly rich period in the history of Western European art.

MEDALS

One of the most distinctive new artistic forms to emerge in Renaissance Italy was the portrait medal, a small, generally two-sided disk that featured a portrait of the patron or the sitter on the face (obverse) of the medal with an inscription of the sitter's name, rank, and title. The imagery on the reverse consisted of a heraldic or symbolic device (*impresa*), a shield with a coat-of-arms, or an allegory or narrative scene of a particular historical event that was intended to convey an aspect of the sitter's character or distinguishing acts.[15]

The majority of Italian Renaissance and Baroque medals were made from bronze or brass because of the latter's durability, the local availability of its ingredients (copper and tin), and the ease with which it could be cast; other, less frequently used materials included gold, silver, and lead. From the fifteenth century through the first half of the sixteenth century, medals were produced by two different methods. To make a cast medal, an artisan would pour molten metal into concave molds of the obverse and reverse faces of the medal, then join them; a struck medal was the result of impressing two engraved metal dies onto a blank disk of a softer metal.[16] Cast medals were more refined in appearance than struck medals from this period because their surfaces were chastened with a chisel or file to enhance details and remove minor imperfections, then polished and lacquered to improve color. Both types of medals were produced in great quantities, and it was not uncommon for subsequent copies, known as aftercasts, to be made using molds of the originals for the casting process. At the beginning of the sixteenth century, the screw press, adapted from machinery for the printing trade, was introduced for striking medals. The new process embossed both sides of the soft medal blank more consistently and with less effort and allowed for higher relief and more multiples. Thereafter, striking using the screw press became the predominant means of medal production in Europe until the mid-nineteenth century.

The development and popularity of the portrait medal in Renaissance Italy arose from humanists' high valuation of individual character and achievement, a perspective that gradually infiltrated contemporary society. Although Renaissance portrait medals were certainly influenced by the format and imagery of ancient Roman coins, they differ significantly in terms of patronage and function.[17] Whereas the Roman Senate and emperors commissioned coinage with imperial portraits for monetary exchange, the patrons of Renaissance portrait medals were private individuals, elite members of society who sought to publicize their political power, proclaim their accomplishments, commemorate a momentous event in their life, and, above all, ensure immortality for themselves or on behalf of their patrons or loyal friends.

Renaissance medals were small, easy to transport, and eminently collectible. Beginning in the fifteenth century, noblemen, scholars, and wealthy patricians assembled collections of portrait medals of important contemporaries, historical personages, and friends to demonstrate their learning, refinement, and judgment.[18] Medals were often exchanged among social equals, presented in recognition of another's achievements or to show respect to one's patrons, and given as intimate gifts to convey feelings of friendship and love.[19] Renaissance portrait medals were housed in chests and cabinets alongside collections of antique gems, cameos, and coins.[20] They were buried in the foundations of buildings, placed in tombs, displayed in scholars' studies, attached to walls, and affixed to furniture.

Although several examples of Italian portrait medals date to the late fourteenth century, the genre was established as a permanent art form in the late 1430s by the northern Italian artist Antonio di Puccio (Pisano), called Pisanello (ca. 1395 – ca. 1455).[21] Pisanello's first medal, which he made as a commercial venture, commemorated the visit of the Byzantine Emperor John VIII Palaiologos to Italy to attend the Council of Ferrara-Florence of ca. 1438/39 that brought together representatives of the Western and Eastern churches. A bust-length portrait of Palaiologos, in profile, appears on the obverse of the large medal, and the reverse includes a second image of the emperor, on horseback, halted while hunting, to pray before a cross in the wilderness.[22] The impact of this work was enormous, leading to commissions for similar medals by Pisanello; the replication of the Byzantine emperor's portrait in other works of sculpture, painting, and engraving; and, most important, the establishment of the popularity of the portrait medal throughout Italy.

The early portrait medals in the Middeldorf Collection selected for this exhibition illustrate the typical imagery, range of artistic quality, and widespread production of medals in fifteenth-century Italy. Coincidentally, the earliest medal in the exhibition also commemorates the Council of Ferrara-Florence, but neither its artist nor its patron is known.[23] Probably produced in Florence ca. 1440, the bronze medal (fig. 2) depicts Pope Eugenius IV enthroned with a crucifix in his lap, flanked by the papal keys and a shield with his family's coat-of-arms, inscribed with his name and the date 1439; on the reverse, Emperor John VIII Palaiologos and the Armenian Patriarch are shown kneeling in the presence of Saint Peter in the heavens. One of only two surviving medals with this specific imagery, this rare work has a somewhat rough appearance, which suggests it may be a poorly executed aftercast of a cast or struck original.

An early admirer of Pisanello's medals, Matteo de' Pasti (active 1441 – 1467/68) worked as a manuscript illuminator,

FIG. 2: *Florence, ca. 1440, medal of Pope Eugenius IV and the Council of Florence (obverse). IUAM, 87.26.2.53.*

painter, architect, and medallist in Venice, Verona, Ferrara, and Rimini. Matteo became a friend and counselor to the *condottiere* Sigismondo Pandolfo Malatesta (1417–1468), lord of Rimini and Fano, who entrusted him with the supervision of architectural projects in the Malatesta lands. To ensure the perpetuation of his name, fame, and important projects, Sigismondo commissioned a large number of portrait medals that were widely distributed and concealed within the structures of the Tempio Malatestiano as well as his Riminese castle and other castles in his territory. Many of his medals bear the date 1446, which is not the date of production but the momentous year when he consolidated political power, dedicated his new castle in Rimini, and secured Isotta degli Atti as his mistress (and later, wife). Matteo's medal of Sigismondo in the Middeldorf

FIG. 3: *Matteo de' Pasti (active 1441–1467/68), medal of Sigismundo Pandolfo Malatesta, 1446 (obverse).* IUAM, *87.26.2.51.*

Collection (fig. 3) depicts him in court dress, but the inscription with his name and title identifies him as captain general of the Holy Roman Church.[24] Heraldic devices decorate the reverse of the medal: a helmet with a coronet, an elephant-head crest, mantling, and a tilted shield with the monogram SI (Sigismondo and Isotta). The elephant was a favorite Malatesta emblem that symbolized regal strength and the immortality conferred by fame.[25]

A medal dated 1465, made in Rome, depicts Pope Paul II (Pietro Barbo; 1417–1471) in a bust-length profile portrait that was reused on other medals of the sitter (fig. 4).[26] Paul II was an enormously wealthy antiquarian from Venice who assembled an outstanding collection of ancient coins, gems, cameos, and intaglios in his medieval palace, the Palazzo Venezia in Rome. (He is also generally

FIG. 4: *Rome, medal of Pope Paul II, 1465 (obverse).* IUAM, *87.26.2.52.*

credited with commissioning the earliest examples of small-scale replicas of these antique originals, today known as plaquettes, a genre of Renaissance collectibles discussed later in this volume.) Echoing the tradition of depicting buildings on coins, the Palazzo Venezia appears on the reverse of the medal to publicize the fact that it became the official papal residence upon Paul's elevation to the papacy, in 1464. Hundreds of copies of this medal were placed in the foundations of the building as it was renovated.

Another early medal in the Middeldorf Collection (fig. 5), by an anonymous designer working in Florence in the 1470s, posthumously celebrates the wealthy banker Cosimo de' Medici (1389–1464) as the father of the city (*pater patriae*), a title awarded to him in 1465; the inscription on the medal repeats the one on Cosimo's floor tomb by Verrocchio, in the crossing of San Lorenzo.[27] Cosimo is portrayed on the

FIG. 5: *Florence, ca. 1470s, medal of Cosimo de' Medici (obverse).* IUAM, *87.26.2.127.*

obverse wearing a flat cap and plain coat, the clothing of a modest Florentine citizen. On the reverse is an unprecedented representation of Florence (Florentia), personified as a woman dressed in antique-style clothing seated above a yoke, an emblem of the Medici family implying their service to the city; she holds an orb (a traditional symbol of power) and a triple olive branch symbolizing peace.

The designers of most early medals were generally professional, multitalented artists for whom the creation of medals was only one aspect of their careers. But by the late fifteenth century, amateurs, generally scholars and diplomats, with little artistic training, if any, began to design portrait medals. One such individual was the aristocratic humanist Giovanni di Salvatore Filangieri of Naples, called Candida (ca. 1445/50 – 1498/99?), who served as the secretary to the duke of Burgundy, Charles the Bold, from

1472 to 1477, frequently traveling on diplomatic missions to Italy and Germany. Upon the duke's death, Candida became secretary to Charles's daughter, Mary of Burgundy (1457–1482), the duchess of Burgundy and countess of Flanders, and her husband, Maximilian of Austria (born 1459; Holy Roman Emperor, 1493–1519). In 1480, Candida moved to France, where he served as a counselor to Charles VII and ambassador to the Holy See. Candida appears to have designed very few medals; one accepted by scholars as his work and representing Maximilian and Mary is in the Middeldorf Collection (fig. 6).[28] The medal is undated, but the youthful appearance of the couple suggests that it was made on the occasion of their wedding, in 1477, and certainly before Candida departed their employ. Their union, which ended after only five years when Mary was thrown from a horse and killed, was considered the marriage of the century as she was the richest heiress in Europe and Maximilian was the son and heir of the Holy Roman Emperor. Ironically, given her nobility and wealth, she is shown on the reverse of the medal dressed simply in a plain dress with a U-shaped neckline, her hair gathered in a loose knot at the back of her head; the couple's monogram, consisting of two interlocked M's under a crown, appears to the left. Maximilian, on the obverse of the medal, has delicately defined, shoulder-length wavy hair secured by a twisted fillet and wreath perhaps made from myrtle leaves, a plant traditionally associated with love and marriage.

In the sixteenth century, the overall scale of Italian medal production expanded; the size of individual editions increased and medals were distributed to larger audiences, due in large part to the fact that more rulers and cities now recognized the propagandistic value of the portrait medal and used it as a tool of political power. With the introduction and widespread dissemination of the new technology of the screw press, which

FIG. 6: *Giovanni Candida (Giovanni di Salvatore Filangieri; ca. 1445/50–1498/99?), medal of Maximilian I and Mary of Burgundy, ca. 1477–78 (obverse).* IUAM, 87.26.2.47.

accommodated the production of medals in greater quantities, die-engravers at official city mints, rather than professional artists, were entrusted more often with the production of medals; in many instances, this change in practice resulted in a noticeable decline in the quality of struck medals, regardless of the source of the design.

Sixteenth-century portrait medals followed the pictorial traditions established in the previous century, consisting of a bust portrait of the sitter, generally in profile, with identifying inscriptions on the obverse and symbolic or allegorical imagery referring to the sitter's character on the reverse. Reflecting the gradual growth of female patronage in the course of the Renaissance, there are more women represented on sixteenth-century medals than on fifteenth-century ones, although their portraits continued

FIG. 7: *Pastorino de Pastorini (ca. 1508–1592), medal of Ludovico Ariosto (obverse).*
IUAM, 87.26.2.60.

to be much less common than those of men. It became fashionable in the sixteenth century to wear medals close to the body, suspended from chains around the neck.

Given Professor Middeldorf's research interests and many years living in Florence, it is not surprising that his medal collection includes a large number of sixteenth- and seventeenth-century portrait medals of members of the ruling Medici family, designed by a succession of outstanding medallists and produced by the city's mint. One such artist was Pastorino de' Pastorini (ca. 1508–1592), who designed more than two hundred high-quality medals over the course of his long and prolific career in Florence and for mints throughout Italy. His fashionable style is represented in the Middeldorf Collection by a medal (fig. 7), probably made in the 1530s, of the famous Ferrarese poet Ludovico

Ariosto (1474–1533), author of the celebrated epic *Orlando Furioso*, published in Ferrara in 1516 and dedicated to the poet's patron, Cardinal Ippolito d'Este.[29] On the medal, Ariosto wears a laurel crown indicative of his status as a poet. The reverse depicts the *impresa* of bees being driven from the hive after producing honey, alluding to Ariosto's displeasure with his compensation for *Orlando Furioso* and his dismissal by the cardinal from the Ferrarese court, in 1518.

The Florentine Domenico de' Vetri (after 1480 – ca. 1547) worked as a gem cutter and medallist primarily for the Medici family. His two medals of Duke Cosimo I in the Middeldorf Collection (figs. 8 and 9), ca. 1540, demonstrate the frequent practice of reusing a sitter's portrait; both medals feature more or less the same image of Cosimo in armor, one without a beard and one with a modest beard.[30] The reverses illustrate the important influence of classical history and myth on the iconography of Renaissance art and thought. One medal features the astrological sign for Capricorn, a goat, with the stars of Ariadne, the wife of Dionysius, a device of Augustus Caesar's that Cosimo I adopted to link himself and his rule with this auspicious antique ancestry. The other medal shows the figure of Hygeia (goddess of health and daughter of the god of medicine, Asclepius) holding a bowl and feeding a snake; together with the inscription "SALVS PVBLICA" ("public health/welfare"), the image implies the well-being of the Florentine duchy under the rule of Cosimo I.

Two later medals of Cosimo I (figs. 10 and 11) by the sculptor and medallist Pier Paolo Galeotti (1520–1584), a student and collaborator of the famous goldsmith and sculptor Benvenuto Cellini, show a slightly older duke, bearded and again wearing armor, emphasizing his political and military power.[31] On the reverse of the medal in figure 11 is a view of the Uffizi and the Palazzo Vecchio with a statue of Justice in the foreground; this

FIG. 8: *Domenico de' Vetri (after 1480–ca. 1547), medal of Duke Cosimo I de' Medici, ca. 1540 (obverse).* IUAM, *87.26.2.59.*

FIG. 9: *Domenico de' Vetri, medal of Duke Cosimo I de' Medici, ca. 1540 (obverse).* IUAM, *87.26.2.65.*

FIG. 10: *Pier Paolo Galeotti, called Romano (1520–1584), medal of Grand Duke Cosimo I de' Medici, 1569 (obverse).* IUAM, *87.26.2.46.*

FIG. 11: *Pier Paolo Galeotti, medal of Duke Cosimo I de' Medici, ca. 1561 (obverse).* IUAM, *87.26.2.58.*

31

medal was made to commemorate the construction of the Uffizi, which served as the ducal offices, and copies were placed in the building's foundation. The reverse of the other medal, which includes the shield of arms with Medici *palle* (balls) surmounted by the grand-ducal crown and the Order of the Golden Fleece below, advertises Cosimo's recent acquisition of the title of grand duke of Tuscany, which Pope Pius V bestowed on him in 1569.

Cosimo I's beloved wife, Eleonora of Toledo (1522–1562), the mother of eleven children, was the daughter of the viceroy of Naples for the Spanish Royal House. She is the subject of a medal (fig. 12) of ca. 1551 by Domenico (1520–1590) and Gianpaolo Poggini (1518–1582), brothers who were gem engravers and goldsmiths at the Medici court in the 1550s and 1560s.[32] Eleonora, whom the duke had married for love in 1539, when she was seventeen years old, was renowned for her beauty and fashionably luxurious attire; she appears here as a mature woman wearing a brocaded dress open at the bodice to reveal a lace chemise. The reverse illustrates her *impresa* of a peahen protecting six young under its spread wings, inscribed with the motto "CVM PVDORE LAETA FOECVNDITAS" ("with modesty, joyful fecundity"), extolling her virtues as a praiseworthy wife and mother.

A second medal by the Pogginis in the Middeldorf Collection (fig. 13) commemorates the marriage in 1565 of Francesco I (the son of Cosimo I and Eleonora), who became the second grand duke of Tuscany upon his father's death, in 1574, and Archduchess Joanna of Austria, on the reverse.[33] Although their heads are shown in profile, their bodies are presented in three-quarter view, perhaps to display their elegant clothing more effectively. Francesco, whose appearance recalls his father's, wears a lace ruff and armor decorated with scales, a mask on the breastplate, and a lion on the shoulder piece.

FIG. 12: *Domenico Poggini (1520–1590) and Gianpaolo Poggini (1518–1582), medal of Princess Eleonora of Toledo, ca. 1551 (obverse).* IUAM, 87.26.2.62.

FIG. 13: *Domenico and Gianpaolo Poggini, medal of Duke Francesco I de' Medici and Archduchess Joanna of Austria, 1565 (obverse).* IUAM, 87.26.2.71.

33

Gaspare Mola (ca. 1580–1640), medal of Grand Duke Cosimo II de' Medici, 1618 (obverse). IUAM, 87.26.2.89.

Joanna wears a mantle over a dress with a high neck-line, a pearl necklace, and her hair pulled back and covered by jeweled (possibly pearl-encrusted) netting.

Three seventeenth-century medals of the later Medici grand dukes — Ferdinand I (1549–1609), brother and successor of Francesco I; Ferdinand I's son Cosimo II (1590–1621); and Cosimo III (1642–1723), father of the last duke of Tuscany — exemplify the traditions of representation associated with the duke's portrayal and the continuing importance of portrait medals in promoting political unity and regard for Medici rule both inside and outside the borders of Florence's domains.[34] The portrait medal of Grand Duke Cosimo III (fig. 14), dated 1666, by Gaspare Morone-Mola, has the novel subject matter on the reverse of a three-masted ship on a rough sea, with four

FIG. 14: *Gaspare Morone-Mola (active 1627–1669), medal of Grand Duke Cosimo III de' Medici, 1666 (obverse)*. IUAM, 87.26.2.94.

prominent stars in the sky. These stars, known as the Medici *stele*, represent the moons of Jupiter that Galileo discovered in 1609 and named after Cosimo II and his three brothers. Following the papacy's condemnation of Galileo in 1663, pictorial representations of the stars were banned, but the Medici employed them later in the century on medals.[35] The inscription "CERTA.FVLGENT.SIDERA" derives from the Roman poet Horace's ode *Ortum* (2.16): "Peace the sailor prays, caught in a storm on the open Aegean, when dark-clad clouds have hid the moon and the stars shine [*fulgent sidera*] no longer certain." The implied message is that the Florentine ship of state is indeed peaceful in the capable hands of Cosimo III and the Medici family.

Francesco Redi (1626–1697) of Arezzo was a poet, scientist, and chief physician to Ferdinand II and Cosimo III.

Cosimo III commissioned his court artist, Massimiliano Soldani Benzi (1656–1740), to design three different medals in 1684, in recognition of Redi's service to the Medici and his many interests and accomplishments. The medal selected for this exhibition (fig.15), one of two from the Redi series in the Middeldorf Collection, illustrates on its reverse Redi's command of science and medicine in an allegorical scene of Minerva, the goddess of wisdom, uncovering a personification of Nature, flanked by a serpent and stag and seated in front of a classical temple, the architrave of which is inscribed "SALVTI" ("health").[36]

Known for its textile manufacturing (including woolen cloths, luxury silks, and cottons) and metalwork (especially armor and armaments), Milan was one of the few vibrant commercial cities in Renaissance Italy. Among the many artists attracted to the brilliant Milanese court in this period was the prolific sculptor, medallist, coin engraver, and goldsmith Leoni Leone (ca.1509–1590). Following his early peripatetic career working in Venice, Padua, Urbino, Rome (where he was imprisoned by the papacy), and Genoa, Leone was appointed master of the imperial mint in Milan in 1542. Recommended by the imperial governor of Milan, Ferrante Gonzaga, Leone received many commissions for medals and sculpture for the Holy Roman Emperor and king of Spain, Charles V (1530–1558), and other members of the Hapsburg family. (In recognition of Leone's work for the royal family, he was made an imperial knight.) The large one-sided bronze medal by Leone in the Middeldorf Collection (fig.16) of Jupiter Thundering Against the Giants, is the reverse of a medal cast in 1549 for Charles V to commemorate his military victory at Muhlberg, Germany, two years earlier and, more important, to celebrate the triumph of the Catholic monarchy over the Protestant forces of the Lutheran League.[37] The composition of this colorful episode from classical

FIG. 15: *Massimiliano Soldani Benzi (1656–1740), medal of Francesco Redi, 1684 (obverse).* IUAM, 87.26.2.111.

FIG. 16: *Leone Leoni (ca. 1509–1590), medal of Jupiter Thundering Against the Giants, 1549.* IUAM, 87.26.2.49.

FIG. 17: *Giovanni dal Cavino (1500–1570), medal of Emperor Septimius Severus, mid-16th century (obverse).* IUAM, *87.26.2.54.*

FIG. 18: *Giovanni dal Cavino (1500–1570), medal of Empress Annia Galeria Faustina, mid-16th-century (obverse).* IUAM, *87.26.2.56.*

mythology derives directly from Perino del Vaga's ceiling fresco of the Fall of the Giants in the Sala dei Giganti of the Palazzo dei Principe (formerly Villa Doria), Genoa, painted ca. 1527–33 for Leone's former patron, Admiral Andrea Doria (1466/8–1560). It was Doria who arranged for the artist's release from the galley-service to which he had been condemned by Pope Leo III.[38] From 1528 until his death, Andrea Doria was Charles V's naval commander in the Mediterranean and his most important ally in Italy.

From the time of the earliest medals through the seventeenth century, designers and their clients were influenced to varying degrees by the style and imagery of antique Roman coins. Among Renaissance medallists, Giovanni di Bartolommeo dal Cavino, called Giovanni Cavino (1500–1570), of Padua, is best known for his medals of Roman emperors made in emulation of the antique. Working in the circle of the most learned men of Padua, scholars of antiquity and collectors of ancient coins, Cavino was not a forger but a skilled imitator whose medals were never exact reproductions of the Roman originals.[39] The Middeldorf medal (fig. 17) of Emperor Septimius Severus wearing armor and crowned with laurel exemplifies Cavino's skills as a medallist; on the reverse, a standing nude figure of Mars, the Roman god of war, holds a spear and shield with armor at his side.[40] The Middeldorf Collection is fortunate to have one of Cavino's few medals of a woman, Empress Annia Galeria Faustina (fig. 18), who was married to her cousin Marcus Aurelius; on the reverse of the medal, the empress appears among a crowd making a sacrifice at an altar in front of a circular temple (perhaps the Temple of Vesta in Rome).[41]

Cavino's medal (fig. 19) of Giovanni Melsi (d. 1589) of Udine, a jurist and member of a charitable organization, illustrates that the demand for medals was not solely the prerogative of the powerful.[42] In a similar fashion to the content and style of medals of more famous sitters, Melsi's portrait has a distinct antiquarian character; moreover, on the reverse, the artist employs classical imagery to convey a sense of the sitter's generous character by depicting him as Genius, the ancient Roman protector and guardian of people's spirits, sacrificing at an altar and holding a cornucopia, symbolizing beneficence.

In the late sixteenth century, a small group of highly original artists working in and around the northern Italian city of Reggio-Emilia created large, mainly single-faced medals of lead that departed from the stylistic traditions previously associated with the portrait medal; one of the outstanding features of these medals is the amount of attention devoted to details of the sitter's clothing. Very little is known about the presumed creators, Agostino and Alessandro Ardenti, or the man portrayed on the large (originally gilded) silver medal in the Middeldorf Collection (fig. 20), inscribed with the name Pietro Machiavelli of Lugo, a small town in the same region as Reggio-Emilia.[43] From the valuable materials employed in the manufacture of the medal and the elegant clothing and jewelry of the sitter (who wears a pinky ring), one may assume that Pietro was a wealthy gentleman of refined taste. If the plant he is holding is a pomegranate, a fruit that in a Christian context represents the hope for resurrection, the medal may have been made after his death.

Another late-sixteenth–century medal in the Middeldorf Collection (fig. 21), tentatively assigned to a group of Emilian medallists referred to as Bombarda (active 1540–1575), bears the provocative, bust-length portrait of Violenta Brasavola, wife of the Ferrarese physician, poet, and historian Giambattista Nicolucci, known as Pigna.[44] She wears a diaphanous blouse with a vertical slash in her left sleeve; the other sleeve has partially slipped off her right shoulder to reveal her breast; a tight sash beneath her breasts further draws attention to her

FIG. 19: *Giovanni dal Cavino, medal of Giovanni Melsi, 1560s (obverse).*
IUAM, *87.26.2.45.*

FIG. 20: *Agostino and Alessandro Ardenti (active, second half of the 16th century),*
medal of Pietro Macchiavelli, late 16th century (obverse). IUAM, *87.26.2.61.*

FIG. 21: *Bombarda (Giovanni Battista Cambi?, active 1540–1582?), medal of Violenta Brasavola Pigna (Nicolucci), third quarter of the 16th century (obverse).* IUAM, 87.26.2.72.

FIG. 22: *Gaspare Morone-Mola (active 1627–1669), medal of Pope Alexander VII, 1657 (obverse).* IUAM, 87.26.2.79.

pulchritude. Violenta's hair is elaborately arranged in tight curls and braids intertwined with a small veil knotted at the back of her head. Her jewelry includes a double strand of pearls, an earring, and what appear to be ornamental clips in her hair. The distinct similarity of this image to others attributed to the Bombarda featuring more or less the same physical features, elements of costume, and air of artificiality reveals it as a stereotypical portrayal of feminine beauty rather than an accurate likeness.[45]

The illustrious tradition of quality medal-making in Italy continued into the seventeenth century, as in the case of Gaspare Mola's medal of Grand Duke Ferdinand I de' Medici of 1608. After time at the mints in Florence, Mantua, Modena, and several others in northern Italy, Mola settled in Rome, where he served as papal mint master from 1625 to 1639. His nephew Gaspare Morone-Mola (active 1627–1669) joined him in partnership in 1637 and succeeded his uncle as engraver to the papal mint. Between 1640 and 1669, Morone-Mola produced a large number of medals and coins for four successive popes, including the stupendous, gilded bronze portrait medal of Pope Alexander VII from 1657 in the Middeldorf Collection (fig. 22).[46] The reverse of the medal presents a bird's-eye view of Saint Peter's and the colonnade designed by Gianlorenzo Bernini ca. 1656 and was made to commemorate the creation of the piazza.

Other than the papacy, Queen Christina of Sweden (1626–1689), was the most avid client of portrait medals in seventeenth-century Rome. A convert to Catholicism who had abdicated her throne and permanently settled in the city as of 1655, Christina, a well-educated woman and collector of ancient coins and gems, commissioned thirty-seven medals of herself out of the more than one hundred she had planned as a history of her life. The Florentine sculptor, goldsmith, and medallist Massimiliano

FIG. 23: *Giovanni Battista Gugliemada (?) (active 1665–1689), medal of Queen Christina of Sweden, 1680s (obverse).* IUAM, *87.26.2.101.*

Soldani Benzi, whose medal of Francesco Redi for Grand Duke Cosimo III of Tuscany was discussed above, designed at least six of these medals. Considered the last of the great Florentine Renaissance bronze artists, Soldani was sent to Rome in 1678 by the grand duke to perfect his medal-making skills. It was there, in 1681, that Soldani created the portrait medals of the former queen and her papal liaison Cardinal Decio Azzolino. The Middeldorf medal (fig. 23) of Queen Christina of Sweden shows the queen as an idealized beauty in the guise of a classical muse crowned with laurel.[47] The reverse, inscribed, "FORTIS. ET.FELIX" ("strength and good fortune [or happiness]") and "GD" for "Gratia Deo" ("thanks be to God"), features a number of symbolic elements alluding to Christina's attributes as a ruler; despite her abdication of the throne of

FIG. 24: *Giovanni Martino Hamerani (1646–1705), medal of Prince Livio Odescalchi, 1689 (obverse). IUAM, 87.26.2.95.*

Sweden, she still behaved like a queen, engaging in unsuccessful political maneuvers to obtain the thrones of Naples in 1656 and Poland in 1668. The lion with eleven stars on its body is the constellation Leo, associated with the qualities of royalty, eminence, and authority; the rudder represents skillful guidance; the globe crossed with two bands is an astrological symbol for happiness; and the cornucopia implies the virtues of generosity and beneficence. Although designed by Soldani, the actual die for the medal was cut by an associate, Gugliemada (active 1665–1689), and struck in the papal mint under the control of the master of the mint, Giovanni Martino Hamerani (1646–1705).

Hamerani was a medallist and coin engraver of Bavarian ancestry who was part of a family dynasty of medal makers working primarily in Rome from the mid-seventeenth

45

through the eighteenth century. He designed a large bronze disk of Prince Livio Odescalchi (1652–1713), duke of Bracciano, another outstanding example of the high quality of Roman medals from this period in the Middledorf Collection (fig. 24).[48] The elegant sitter was the nephew of Pope Innocent XI (Benedetto Odescalchi) and a *gonfaloniere* (standard bearer) of the Holy Roman Church. He was also a great collector of Roman antiquities, which he acquired from Queen Christina. The striking image on the reverse of the medal — a radiant sun with a human face rising over the horizon and shedding its light on Italy and Austria, with the inscription "NON NVVS SED NOVITER" ("not new but under new auspices") — refers to the fact that Odescalchi was a prince of the Holy Roman Empire, appointed by Emperor Leopold I, under whose reign Austria had emerged as a European power.

PLAQUETTES

The modern term "plaquette" refers to a wide variety of mostly small, low-relief sculptures generally made of bronze or sometimes lead, which were produced in multiple copies from a cast or struck from a die, primarily by fifteenth- and sixteenth-century Italian craftsmen.[49] Plaquettes are generally round, rectangular, or oval and decorated on only one side with historical or mythological narrative scenes, the majority based on antique sources.[50] The back of the relief is usually flat, or indented if the repoussé technique has been used. Plaquettes were created primarily as collectibles or parts of desk ornaments (inkwells, sandboxes, and caskets) and liturgical objects (tabernacles, portable altars, paxes, and candlesticks).[51] In the Renaissance, the same elite circle of scholars, clerics, noblemen, and other educated individuals who assembled collections of medals and ancient coins also acquired so-called reproductive plaquettes.[52] In the case of decorative plaquettes, it was not uncommon for the small reliefs originally made for one purpose to be later recast or reused in another context; moreover, many piercings found today in plaquettes indicate later adaptions in their function or display.

Most scholars believe the plaquette emerged as an independent art form in Rome in the 1440s and 1450s (around the same time as the portrait medal) as an outgrowth of the interest in archaeological classicism on the part of humanists and other scholars.[53] The wealthy Venetian cardinal Pietro Barbo (later Pope Paul II), whose portrait medal was discussed earlier, is generally credited with commissioning the first plaquettes, to reproduce ancient Greek and Roman engraved gems in his collection.[54] The Middeldorf plaquette of Hermaphroditus being fanned and serenaded by several winged putti (fig. 25), derives from an antique cameo today in the Museo Archeologico, Florence, that once belonged to Cardinal Barbo.[55]

In Rome in the same period, the Florentine architect and sculptor Antonio di Pietro di Averlino, known as Filarete (ca. 1400–1469), was at work on the bronze doors for Saint Peter's (completed in 1445), where he included many isolated small, low reliefs. Scholars have suggested that Filarete's episodic method of modeling and casting led him to develop the plaquette as an autonomous work of art.[56] Whether or not Filarete was responsible for the many plaquettes that Middeldorf and others have attributed to him, both types of plaquettes — the reproductive and those with original (secular) subject matter — came into being in Rome more or less simultaneously. The earliest plaquettes with Christian content (specifically, the image of the Virgin and Child) may have been introduced by the Florentine sculptor Donatello (ca. 1386–1466) and his followers, who brought the genre to northern Italy during his sojourn in Padua from 1443 to 1454.[57] Production of plaquettes flourished in Rome and Mantua from ca. 1475 to ca. 1525; thereafter, the quality of execution and originality of the designs declined to the point that demands for this art form ceased by the end of the sixteenth century.

One of the most talented artists of the fifteenth century, who responded to the antiquarian taste for plaquettes in Padua from ca. 1465 to ca. 1475, was Giovanni Fonduli (ca. 1430–ca. 1497), formerly known as Master I O. F. F. (the initials found on a half dozen compositions attributed to him). Produced in a variety of formats to accommodate different decorative functions, Fonduli's designs for plaquettes were extremely popular and reproduced extensively, including by other artists in various other media. The gilded bronze plaquette (fig. 26) of the Judgment of Paris in the Middeldorf Collection is probably a modern aftercast of Fonduli's original, which survives in numerous copies.[58]

FIG. 25: *Italy, 15th century, plaquette of Hermaphroditus with three putti.*
IUAM, 87.26.2.8.

FIG. 26: *Modern aftercast of Master I O. F. F. (Giovanni Fonduli, ca. 1430–ca. 1497),*
plaquette of the Judgment of Paris. IUAM, 87.26.2.7.

FIG. 27: *Modern aftercast of Master I O. F. F. (Giovanni Fonduli), plaquette of Hercules and the Nemean Lion.* IUAM, 87.26.2.9.

In light of the significance of this famous episode from Greek mythology — Paris's choice of Venus as the winner of a beauty contest with Juno and Minerva precipitated the Trojan War — this plaquette with Fonduli's design was often attached to the pommel of swords and daggers.[59] Two other modern overcasts of plaquettes by Fonduli in the Middeldorf Collection illustrate another, similarly popular subject matter of Renaissance art and literature: the twelve labors of Hercules.[60] Ultimately derived from compositions found on antique gems, the scene of Hercules and the Nemean Lion (fig. 27) depicts the nude hero wrestling the beast. The composition of this relief survives in various forms in a variety of shapes, again reflecting the multiple ways in which Renaissance consumers used plaquettes.

FIG. 28: *Ulocrino (active ca. 1485), plaquette of the Death of Meleager (recto).*
IUAM, 72.45.

Attributed to another artist working in Padua ca. 1485,
known only by the pseudonym Ulocrino, the rectangular
plaquette (fig. 28) with the Death of Meleager illustrates
the filicide of the Greek hero recounted at length in Ovid's
Metamorphoses (VIII, 270–545).[61] At his birth, the Fates
predicted that Meleager would live only so long as the

brand then on the fire was preserved; his mother Althaea immediately pulled it from the fire and hid it in a chest. Many years later, Meleager, after killing the Calydonian boar, quarreled with his uncles over the prize boar skin and killed them. Althaea was so grieved by her brothers' death that she took the brand from its hiding place and threw it in the fire. Although Meleager was far away, in the forest, he died when the brand was consumed. On the plaquette, the heroic nude figure of Meleager is shown seated on a rock with his left hand on the boar's head. Althaea stands behind her son holding aloft a grotesque mask (possibly representing her grief-stricken state of mind) as she fuels the fire on the altar with the fatal brand. A barren tree in the background of the composition adds to the pathos evoked by the tragic scene. A popular theme on carved Roman tombs, the story of Meleager was known to many Renaissance artists through numerous antique reliefs of the subject.

A contemporary and acquaintance of Michelangelo in Rome, Valerio Belli (ca. 1468–1546) was a gem carver, goldsmith, and medallist whose plaquette designs were often cast directly from his engraved gems. An example of this practice in the Middeldorf Collection is the oval, lead plaquette (fig. 29) with the Roman goddess of good luck and destiny, Fortuna (Fortune), holding a rudder and a serpent.[62] The rudder derives from ancient Roman iconography, where it suggests guidance and good counsel; the snake may be intended as a symbol of good health. A unique plaquette in the Middeldorf Collection (fig. 30), attributed to a follower of Belli, depicts a charming image of Diana, the goddess of the hunt, holding a staff as she strides along a path with a hunting dog by her side.[63]

Two small, sixteenth-century cast bronze reliefs in the Middeldorf Collection, both manufactured in Venice by anonymous designers working in two very different styles and formats, are typical examples of the thousands

FIG. 29: *Valerio Belli (ca. 1468–1546), plaquette of Fortune.* IUAM, 87.26.2.4.

of plaquettes with religious subjects that were made in Italy in this period. The rectangular composition of Saint Jerome in the Wilderness (fig. 31), one of the most popular penitential images in Renaissance art, reflects the work of such contemporary Venetian painters as Giovanni Bellini, Cima da Conegliano, and Bartolomeo Montagna, particularly in regard to the lush appearance of the wilderness landscape where the penitent saint kneels before a crucifix, beating his chest with a rock.[64] Dating later in the century, the small oval plaquette of the Trinity (fig. 32) — the dove

FIG. 30: *After Valerio Belli, plaquette of Diana.* IUAM, *87.26.2.5.*

of the Holy Ghost together with God the Father, who is seated and holding Christ on the Cross — was made to be attached to a larger surface, perhaps as a badge on clothing, mounted on the cover of a religious book or ledger, attached to a piece of furniture or liturgical object.[65]

Middeldorf, who was considered the leading expert on plaquettes of his generation, remarks in a 1948 review, "Plaquettes are a most obstreperous material and often sorely try the patience of a scholar. First there are

FIG. 31: *Venice, early 16th century, plaquette of Saint Jerome in Penitence.*
IUAM, 87.26.2.10.

a great number of them. Then, most of them are unre-
lated; at the same time, they are often linked with works
in other media. Thus, the study of any work in this field
requires the piecing together of innumerable bits of information and involves continuous excursions into the
fields of prints, goldsmithwork [*sic*], cut gems, etc. The
available information, even when properly used, may at
times be less than helpful. . . . There has been much pure
guessing in this field [of scholarship on plaquettes]."[66]

FIG. 32: *Venice, late 16th century, plaquette of the Trinity.* IUAM, *87.26.2.2.*

TEXTILES

From the twelfth to the sixteenth century, Italy was the predominant center of textile weaving in Europe, known for its production of high-quality wool and silk cloth. Its economic development and prosperity relative to other areas in Europe during this period was largely due to the Italian merchant-bankers who financed the manufacture and finishing of luxury fabrics and sold these commodities throughout the Continent. Good cloth was extremely expensive due to the high cost of raw materials and dyestuffs and the fact that production was limited by human-powered looms.[67] Guilds and city governments carefully regulated all aspects of the production of high-quality silk textiles — the silk threads, dyes, and weaving techniques — to protect buyers and to ensure the reputation of the Italian silk industry.[68] Purchased by the wealthiest classes of society to be used for men's and women's clothing, ecclesiastical garments, wall hangings, cloths of honor, upholstery, and diplomatic gifts, luxury textiles represent the most flamboyant aspect of Renaissance conspicuous consumption. Whereas medals and plaquettes were, for the most part, "consumed" privately, items made of expensive wool and silk cloth, especially clothing, were created for public display as prestigious visual signs of social and economic status.

Due to the precious nature and inherent value of Italian Renaissance and Baroque luxury textiles, many were transformed, damaged, or destroyed over the course of time. In the fifteenth and sixteenth centuries, silk fabrics, especially those used for clothing, frequently changed hands; they were sold on the secondhand market and/or donated to the church to be redeployed in liturgical vestments, wall hangings, and cloths of honor.[69] Moreover, textiles made with precious metals were sometimes melted

down to recover the gold and silver used in their manufacture.[70] In the nineteenth century, when it became
fashionable to collect antique fabrics, many valuable textiles were cut into pieces, thereby making it more difficult
to reconstruct their original design, shape, or context.
This fragmentation explains why the surviving fabrics
from this period are primarily ecclesiastical garments and
other assorted textile fragments, such as those assembled
by Ulrich Middeldorf in his collection of "samples."

   The majority of textile fragments in the Middeldorf
Collection are silk. Silk cloth was produced in Italy as early
as the eleventh century but not in large quantities before
the late thirteenth century, at which time Lucca became
the leading center of silk weaving in Europe. When political turmoil led to a steep decline in Lucca's output of
silk fabric, production shifted to Venice, Florence, and
Genoa. Over the next two centuries, other, smaller cities
in central and northern Italy and Spain began making silk
textiles; as the industry developed, technical innovations
and designs spread from one textile center to another.
It is difficult, without external evidence, to differentiate
their production, especially as of the second half of the
sixteenth and seventeenth century, or securely to iden-
tify the place of origin of individual silk textiles because
methods of production, patterns, selvedge colors, and
loom widths were similar throughout the peninsula.[71]

   Under the influence of Oriental silks imported during
the late thirteenth and fourteenth century, the silk in-
dustries of both Italy and Spain developed several new
types of luxury fabrics and weaves: namely, satin, lampas,
and velvet.[72] Satin has a distinctive smooth, glossy surface
because the warp, the vertical threads of the textile, dom-
inates (or in technical terms, "floats over") the weft, the
horizontal threads or filler, with a minimum number of
interlacings between the two. Lampas is a more complex,

compound weave characterized by its contrasting textures
and distinctive patterns. In lampas silks, the ground of the
fabric consists of a main warp and weft combined with
one or more weft-dominant weaves to create a pattern.[73]
A heavier, extremely popular variant of lampas silk, brocatelle, employs silk and linen for the warp and weft of the
ground and silk alone for the warp and weft of the pattern,
thereby creating the appearance that the ground weave
is raised slightly above the pattern weave. Lampas silks
were often brocaded with discontinuous wefts of colored
silks and enriched with gilt or silver metal threads.[74]

Velvet (*velluto* in Italian), the "newest" of the textiles
introduced in this period, is distinguished from all other
fabrics by its surface pile, created in the process of weaving by supplemental pile warps that are raised above the
ground weave and over rods, thereby creating loops.[75] The
rods are removed and additional weft threads are inserted
to secure the loops, which are then left intact or cut in
various ways. In a voided velvet (*velluto raso*, also known as
velluto a inferriata), the pattern of the fabric is created by a
single-height cut pile on a smooth satin ground.[76] Figured
velvets combine cut and uncut velvet pile on a satin or other
ground. The most expensive of silk velvets were multiple-
pile velvets, including ciselé velvet (*velluto cesellato*), where
the uncut piles are higher than the cut piles, and velvet
brocaded with gold (*velluto broccato d'oro*).[77] As of the 1420s,
velvets were produced that incorporated raised loops of
gold or silver above the silk pile; because the gold appeared
as if it were shimmering in the silk background, velvet of
this kind became known as *velluto allucciolato*, literally "lit-up
velvet," from the Italian word for firefly, *lucciolo*. The most
extravagant of all the velvets was *velluto riccio sopra riccio* (loop
over loop velvet), in which the metal loops are at different
heights. Of the three types of Renaissance and Baroque
silk textiles, velvet was the most costly because it required

FIG. 34: *Italy, mid-15th century, textile fragment, cut voided velvet on satin weave ground.* IUAM, 87.26.1.673.

a larger amount of silk than the other two.[78] Not surprisingly, it was the most highly prized luxury fabric in Europe.

The Middeldorf Collection includes a number of good examples of these three types of silk fabrics, produced in Italy and Spain, from the fifteenth through the seventeenth century. Among the earliest samples are seven velvets that exemplify the variety of ways in which the surface pile was treated in the Renaissance and Baroque periods to create elaborate decorative effects. The pile was cut (fig. 33), voided (figs. 34 and 35), cut and uncut (figs. 36–38), and woven at different heights (fig. 39). All of these velvets are shades of red, the most desirable and costly color in this period.[79] Expensive velvets like these were used for clothing of the elite, wall coverings, furnishings, and, especially, liturgical vestments. For example, two large velvet panels in the Middeldorf Collection (fig. 35) once formed the front or back of a chasuble worn by the priest at the celebration of the Catholic Mass.

OPPOSITE, FIG. 33: *Italy, possibly Florence, late 15th century, silk and linen panel, cut velvet.* IUAM, 91.99.

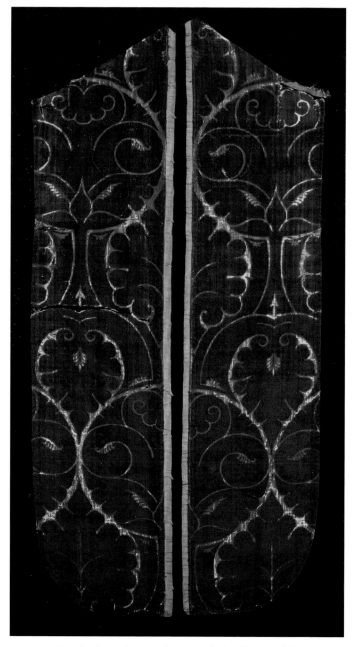

FIG. 35: *Italy, mid- to late 15th century, fragments of a chasuble, cut voided velvet on satin weave ground.* IUAM, *91.108.1-2.*

FIG. 36: *Italy, 15th—16th century, textile fragment, cut and uncut velvet on plain weave ground. IUAM, 87.26.1.672.*

FIG. 37: *Italy, second half of the 16th century, textile fragment, cut and uncut velvet on plain weave ground. IUAM, 87.26.1.4.*

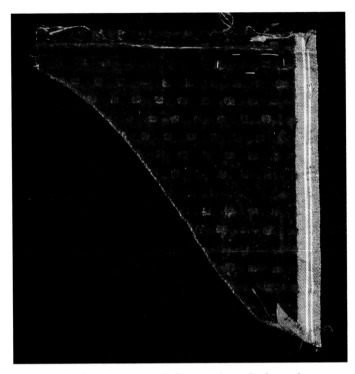

FIG. 39: *Italy, 15th–16th century, textile fragment, pile-on-pile velvet on plain weave ground.* IUAM, *87.26.1.174.*

One of the velvet pieces (fig. 33), originally part of a wall hanging or wall covering, is an excellent example of the extremely popular pomegranate pattern that dominated the production of silk textiles from the mid-fifteenth century through the early seventeenth century. In this early version of the pattern, elaborate foliage and undulating stems accompany the pomegranate. Over the next two centuries, textile designers created countless variations of the pomegranate and other related forms, e.g., the thistle, pineapple, pinecone, and lotus flower. The tapered oval outline of the motif changed from a

OPPOSITE, FIG. 38: *Italy or Spain, 16th century, textile fragment, cut and uncut velvet.* IUAM, *87.26.1.220B.*

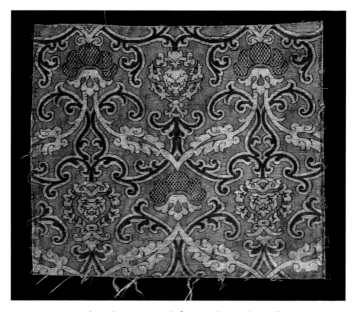

FIG. 40: *Spain, 16th–17th century, textile fragment, lampas, brocatelle.*
IUAM, 87.26.1.943.

free-flowing organic design into a more rigid, formal
arrangement; moreover, the orientation of the repeat
shifted from a diagonal to a vertical or horizontal axis.
The Middeldorf collection includes a number of represen-
tative examples of this evolution in textile design from the
sixteenth and seventeenth century (figs. 37 and 40–44).

As mentioned earlier in this essay, the specific origins of
textiles in this period are not generally known, but there
are exceptions. For example, the silk weavers of Tuscany
specialized in figurative textiles (*tessuti figurati*) with
Christian subject matter, to be incorporated into church
vestments, altar frontals, and liturgical hangings. Four
examples of this type are in the Middeldorf Collection,
all brocatelles dating from the second half of the fifteenth
century (figs. 45–48). The long, wide band with the Man
of Sorrows — Christ standing in his tomb with his back
against the cross (fig. 45) — was probably part of the band,

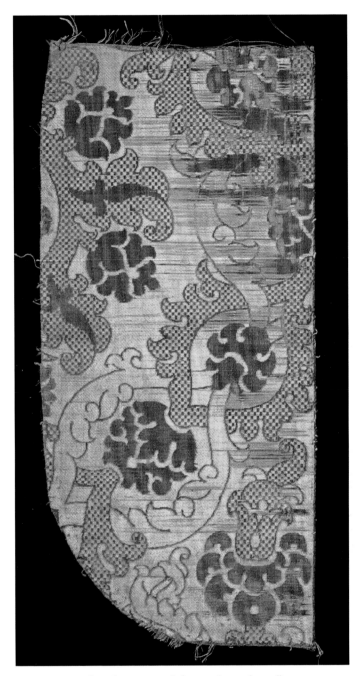

FIG. 41: *Spain, 16th—17th century, textile fragment, lampas, brocatelle.*
IUAM, 87.26.1.1114.

FIG. 42: *Spain, 16th–17th century, chasuble fragment (?), lampas, brocatelle.*
IUAM, 87.26.1.1113.

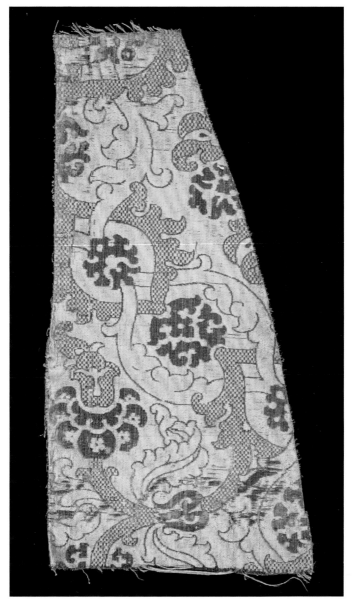

FIG. 43: *Spain, 16th–17th century, textile fragment, lampas, brocatelle.*
IUAM, *87.26.1.924.*

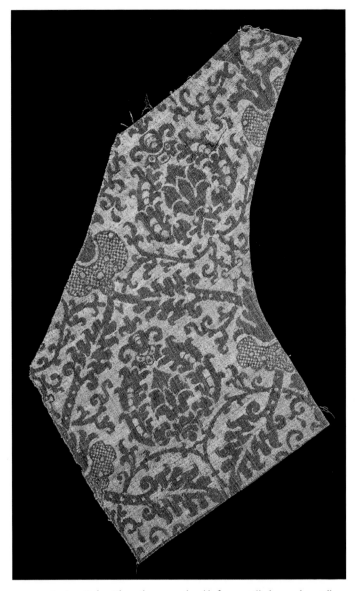

FIG. 44: *Spain or Italy, 16th—17th century, chasuble fragment (?), lampas, brocatelle.* IUAM, *87.26.1.905.*

OPPOSITE, FIG. 45: *Italy, probably Tuscany, second half of the 15th century, orphrey band with Man of Sorrows, lampas, brocatelle.* IUAM, *91.143.*

FIG. 46: *Italy, probably Tuscany, second half of the 15th century, rectangular panel with Annunciation, lampas, brocatelle.* IUAM, *87.26.1.1122.*

known as the *orphrey*, that decorated the liturgical mantle or cloak (cope) worn by the priest or the framing element of an altar frontal. A rectangular panel with the Annunciation (fig. 46) served a similar function as part of the decoration of an altar frontal or as apparel, the decoration placed near the neck, on the sleeves, and above the hem on the front and back of a dalmatic (fig. 49), the vestment worn by the bishop, deacon, and subdeacon.[80]

Two other woven pieces that depict the Assumption of the Virgin (figs. 47 and 48) were once the orphrey band and hood from a cope.[81] Typical of the luxury fabrics employed

OPPOSITE, FIG. 47: *Italy, probably Tuscany, second half of the 15th century, orphrey band with Virgin Giving Her Girdle to Saint Thomas, lampas, brocatelle.* IUAM, *91.148.*

FIG. 48: *Hood of a cope (companion to fig. 46), lampas, brocatelle. IUAM, 91.150.*

for church vestments, the lampas weave is embellished with silvered metal threads (now tarnished). Both pieces depict the Virgin rising to heaven, giving Saint Thomas her belt as a sign of her physical and spiritual assumption, based on the late-thirteenth-century account of the Virgin's life in Jacopus da Voragine's *Golden Legend*. As a subject of religious art and ecclesiastical figurative textiles, the "Virgin of the Holy Girdle" was popular in Tuscany due to the fact that, as of the twelfth century, the relic of the Virgin's belt was housed in the cathedral of Prato.[82]

Beginning in the late sixteenth century, textile weavers in Italy and Spain began to differentiate between the designs and weights of silks depending on their intended

FIG. 49: *Italy, ca. 1450—75, dalmatic. Detroit Institute of Arts, Gift of Mr. and Mrs. Edgar B. Whitcomb. Acc. no. 37.56.*

use. The European fashion for narrowly cut garments, as well as the example of contemporary, imported Persian textiles, resulted in a new taste for small, scattered floral and geometric designs, including branch/sprig, barrette, and S-curved motifs. At the same time, large, bold designs continued to be popular for ecclesiastical garments and furnishings. The range of colors used for silk textiles also expanded from the fifteenth-century palette of red, green, yellow, and blue to include white, garnet, purple, olive green, tones of brown, black, and gray.[83] The wide range of weaves, designs, and color of sixteenth- and seventeenth-century Italian and Spanish fabrics is well represented by the textile fragments in the Middeldorf Collection, including examples

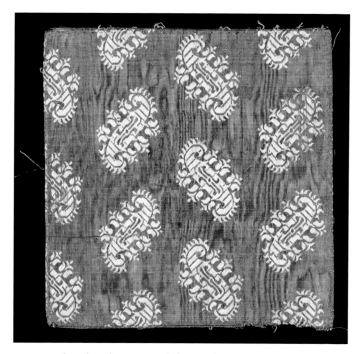

FIG. 50: *Italy, 16th–17th century, textile fragment, lampas.* IUAM, *87.26.1.282.*

of lampas silks of plain weave (figs. 50 and 51), satin weave
embellished with gold metal thread (fig. 52), and a number
of elaborately patterned brocatelles (figs. 40–44 and 53).

In addition to the silks produced for the luxury and
fashion market in the Renaissance and Baroque periods, the Middeldorf Collection includes rare examples of
seventeenth-century, Italian-made woolen (figs. 54–56)
and woolen and linen double cloth (figs. 57 and 58).
Double cloth is a woven textile in which two or more
sets of warp threads and one or more sets of weft or
filling yarns are interconnected to form a two-layered
cloth; it is a sturdy, reversible fabric that often features
complex patterns and surface textures. These fabrics
were employed for clothing and furnishings and constituted the principal textiles of early modern Europe.

FIG. 51: *Italy, 17th century, textile fragment, lampas.* IUAM, *87.26.1.127.*

Interested in all aspects of the history of handicrafts, Middeldorf also collected samples of needlework, including a great number of bobbin laces, and several precious works of embroidery. The earliest is a portion of a

FIG. 52: *Italy, 17th century, textile fragment, satin weave.* IUAM, 87.26.1.132.

FIG. 53: *Spain, 16th–17th century, panel, lampas, brocatelle.* IUAM, 87.26.1.935.

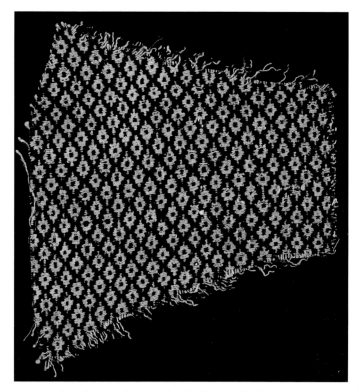

FIG. 54: *Italy, 17th century, fragment of wool and linen double cloth.* IUAM, *87.26.1.56.*

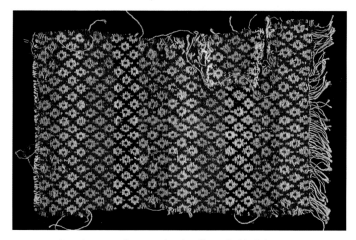

FIG. 55: *Italy, 17th century, fragment of wool and linen double cloth.* IUAM, *87.26.1.57.*

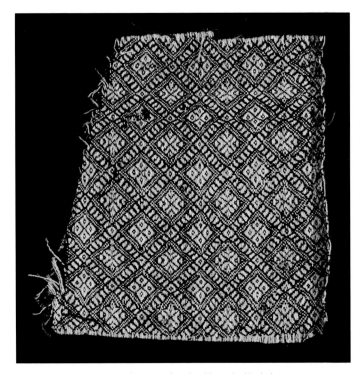

FIG. 56: *Italy, 17th century, fragment of wool and linen double cloth.* IUAM, *87.26.1.58.*

sixteenth-century Italian border (fig. 59) that employs a
technique known as darned netting in which a solid pattern
is embroidered on a ground of open, knotted netting.[84]
In this case, the needle worker used brightly colored silk
threads and gilt and silver yarns on a grid work of red silk
darned stitches. This same technique was used in a second border from seventeenth-century Italy (fig. 60) that
originally may have decorated a pillow, bed linens, a table-
cloth, or another domestic furnishing. The third example
of needlework from the Middeldorf Collection (fig. 61) is
an intact cushion of plain white linen embroidered with
red silk thread with small and large S-shaped motifs and
floral and branch devices, in a style known as redwork;
the outermost border is finished with a braid to which

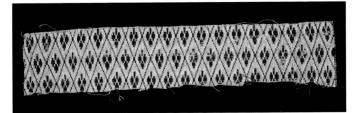

FIG. 57: *Italy, 17th century, fragment of wool and linen double cloth.* IUAM, *87.26.1.53.*

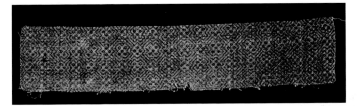

FIG. 58: *Italy, 17th century, fragment of wool and linen double cloth.* IUAM, *87.26.1.60.*

FIG. 59: *Italy, 16th century, section of a border in darned netting.* IUAM, *87.26.1.689.*

FIG. 60: *Italy, 17th century, section of a border in embroidery and darned netting.* IUAM, *87.26.1.763.*

FIG. 61: *England or Italy, early 17th century, cushion with embroidery.*
IUAM, 87.26.1.764.

small-scale toggles are attached. This extremely rare pillow, made in England or Italy in the seventeenth century, would have been used in a domestic setting, probably on a bed.

Middeldorf's approach to collecting was not systematic; he did not have "to have every example of a particular type of medal or brocade from a certain period."[85] Nevertheless, as this brief survey of selected medals, plaquettes, and textiles demonstrates, his collection exemplifies the wide range of artifacts that enhance our understanding of the society and culture of medieval and Renaissance Italy. In his published writings and correspondence, Middeldorf on a number of occasions expressed the importance of such objects to the study and appreciation of past civilizations. Surely, he would be pleased that the collection he so lovingly assembled and shared with his students and visitors to his home continues to this day to enrich the aesthetic experiences of viewers, to impart knowledge, and to stimulate inquiry.

NOTES

1. For the bibliography of Middeldorf's writings, see "Middeldorf, Ulrich," www.khi.fi.it/en/institut/geschichte/index.html.

2. Middeldorf owned Hill's annotated copy of Alfred Armand's *Les médailleurs italiens des XVme et XVIme siècles*, 3 vols. (Paris: E. Plon, 1883–87), which he in turn annotated. The volumes are today in the special collections of the Getty Research Institute Library, Ulrich Alexander Middeldorf Papers (hereafter cited as Middeldorf Papers), 1925–1981, series IV, boxes 39–40.

3. Among his many graduate students were Seymour Slive, Bates Lowry, Peter Selz, Francis Dowley, and Rosalie B. Green.

4. For his obituaries, see John Pope-Hennessy, *Apollo* 117, no. 2 (1983): 420; Herbert Keutner, *Mitteilungen des Kunsthistorischen Institutes in Florenz* 27, no. 3 (1983): 256–60; Gian Carlo Bojani, *Faenza, Bollettino del Museo internazionale delle ceramiche in Faenza* 69, nos. 3–4 (1983): 347–48; and Anthony Radcliffe, *Burlington Magazine* 126, no. 974 (1984): 288–90.

5. Radcliffe, 289.

6. Ulrich Middeldorf, review of *Piccola Biblioteca del Museo delle Ceramiche in Faenza. II: Catalogo delle porcellane del Medici* by Giuseppe Liverani and *Piccola Biloteca del Museo delle Ceramiche in Faenza. III: Rapporti di gusto e influssi di stile fra la pittura e la ceramica faentina del quattrocento* by Rezio Buscaroli, in *Art Bulletin* 20, no. 1 (1938): 117. The collection to which Middeldorf referred, that of Albert Figdor (1843–1927), was one of the largest private collections in Europe, consisting of paintings by old and modern masters, miniatures, sculptures, medieval and Renaissance furniture, textiles, ceramics, gold work, and Judaica. Regarding the collection, see Allan S. Janik and Hans Veigl, *Wittgenstein in Vienna: A Biographical Excursion Through the City and Its History* (New York: Springer, 1998): 176–77. In its focus on the decorative arts of the past, Figdor's collection was typical of the type of collections that became fashionable in the nineteenth century. See Arthur MacGregor, *Curiosity and Enlightenment: Collectors and Collecting from the 16th to the 19th Century* (New Haven, CT: Yale University Press, 2008), 293. Middeldorf probably visited this collection in person sometime before its dispersal in 1930. Middeldorf's belief in the integral relationship between the fine and

decorative arts may have been influenced by the ground-breaking display by Wilhelm von Bode, the director general of the Prussian Museums (1906–1920), of the collection of the Kaiser-Friedrich Museum in Berlin, where paintings, sculpture, furniture, and medals were grouped according to their historical context rather than being separated by medium.

7. Meyric C. Rogers, "The Chicago Meeting of the College Art Association: The Place of Connoisseurship in Art in Universities and Museums with Particular Emphasis on the Minor Arts," *Parnassus* 13, no. 3 (1941): 112.

8. Bruce Cole, foreword to Arne R. Flaten, *Medals and Plaquettes in the Ulrich Middeldorf Collection at the Indiana University Art Museum, 15th to 20th Centuries* (Bloomington: Indiana University Art Museum and Indiana University Press, 2012), x. The Middeldorfs also collected porcelain, tablecloths, *New Yorker* magazine covers, wrapping paper, and novels about art.

9. Ulrich Middeldorf and Oswald Goetz, *Medals and Plaquettes from the Sigmund Morgenroth Collection* (Chicago: Art Institute of Chicago, 1944), xi.

10. Ulrich Middeldorf, review of *Le plachette italiane* by Eugenio Imbert, *Art Bulletin* 30, no. 2 (1948): 151.

11. Cole, in *Medals and Plaquettes*, reports that Middeldorf bought many fabrics from Florentine rag dealers whom he commissioned as his agents.

12. Ulrich Middeldorf, "Überrashungen im Palazzo Pitti," *Pantheon* 32, no. 1 (1947): 18–24; idem, "Statuen und Stoffe," *Pantheon* 35, no. 1 (1977): 10–14; Regarding Middeldorf's interest in textiles as documented in his correspondence, see Perri Lee Roberts, "Ulrich A. Middeldorf (1901–1983) and Textiles," *Getty Research Journal* 5 (2013): 189–96.

13. Letter from Rosalie B. Green to Middeldorf, February 24, 1978, Middeldorf Papers, box 7. Green (1917–2012) was the director of the Index of Christian Art, Princeton University, from 1951 to 1982. She supplied Middeldorf with the photograph of the bust of a lady, attributed to Verrocchio, in the collection of the Princeton Art Museum that he used as an illustration in his article "Statuen und Stoffe."

14. Letter from Middeldorf to Harold B. Burnham, January 29, 1960, Middeldorf Papers, box 7.

15. For recent literature on the Renaissance portrait medal, see *The Currency of Fame: Portrait Medals of the Renaissance*, ed. Stephen K. Scher (New York: Harry N. Abrams, 1994); *Perspectives on the Renaissance Medal*, ed. Stephen K.

Scher (London: Garland, 2000); John Graham Pollard, *Renaissance Medals: Italy*, vol. 1 (Washington, DC: National Gallery of Art, 2007); and Stephen J. Campbell, review of Ulrich Pfisterer, *Lysippus und seine Freunde* and John Graham Pollard, *Renaissance Medals*, *Art Bulletin* 93, no. 1 (2011): 105–8.

16. For a more in-depth discussion of the processes of medal-making in fifteenth- and sixteenth-century Italy, see Scher, *The Currency of Fame*, 13–14.

17. Flaten, *Medals and Plaquettes*, 4. Large numbers of Roman coins were available in Italy at this time and were collected as of the fourteenth century; however, medals were never intended to be copies of these antique prototypes. Campbell, 105.

18. "Through the possession of objects, one physically acquired knowledge, and through their display, one symbolically acquired the honor and reputation that all men of learning cultivated." Paula Findlen, *Possessing Nature: Museums, Collecting, and Scientific Culture in Early Modern Italy* (Berkeley: University of California Press, 1994), 3.

19. On the importance of gift giving among collectors and their patrons, see Findlen, 348.

20. On the display of medals, see Arne E. Flaten, "Identity and the display of *medaglie* in Renaissance and Baroque Europe," *Word & Image* 19, nos. 1–2 (2003): 59–72.

21. The earliest known Renaissance portrait medals were commissioned by Francesco II Novello da Carrara, lord of Treviso and Padua and intimate friend of Petrarch, one of the earliest collectors of Roman coins. In 1390, Francesco II ordered three medals to celebrate his victory over the Milanese, depicting himself and his father in the guise of Roman emperors. For the medals, see Patricia Fortini Brown, *Venice and Antiquity: The Venetian Sense of the Past* (New Haven, CT: Yale University Press, 1996), 96.

22. For the medal, see Scher, *The Currency of Fame*, 44–46.

23. Flaten, *Medals and Plaquettes*, 15, no. 1.

24. Ibid., 17, no. 3.

25. Alison Luchs, in Scher, *The Currency of Fame*, 64.

26. Flaten, *Medals and Plaquettes*, 18, no. 6.

27. Ibid., 16–17, no. 2.

28. Ibid., 19, no. 7.

29. Ibid., 20, no. 10.

30. IUAM acc. nos. 87.26.2.59 and 87.26.2.65. "The condition of the medal [fig. 8] makes it difficult to determine whether this is the younger unbearded Cosimo or the slightly later Cosimo with a modern beard." Ibid., 19–20, nos. 8 and 9.

31. Ibid., 22–23, nos. 13 and 14.

32. Ibid., 21, no. 11.

33. Ibid., 21, no. 12.

34. IUAM acc. nos. 87.26.2.93, 87.26.2.89, and 87.26.2.94. Flaten, *Medals and Plaquettes*, 39, nos. 42 and 43; 46, no. 55.

35. Flaten, *Medals and Plaquettes*, 46.

36. Ibid., 59, no. 82. The snake was an attribute of Asclepius and was therefore associated with healing. According to ancient and medieval bestiaries, the stag was a traditional enemy of the snake; after eating a snake, the stag drinks from a fountain and thereby becomes a young animal again.

37. Ibid., 32, no. 32.

38. For the other medal in the Middeldorf Collection (IUAM acc. no. 87.26.2.44) by Leone, with portraits of the artist and admiral, see ibid., 31, no. 31.

39. Ibid., 25. "In addition, evidence shows that some Renaissance collectors would have known the difference between Cavino's medals and genuine antique coins." Donald Meyers, in Scher, *The Currency of Fame*, 182–83.

40. Flaten, 26, no. 21.

41. Ibid.

42. Ibid., 26, no. 23. The reverse is based on various Roman coin types, particularly those of Nero.

43. Ibid., 32, no. 33.

44. Ibid., 35, no. 35. The obverse of the medal preserves the concave impression of its model. The name of the artists derives from the signature BOM or BOMB[arda] that appears on some seventeen medals, "a number of which portray women dressed as fantasies *all'antica*, often represented as sculptured bust portraits, supported on scrolled brackets." Mary L. Levkott, in Scher, *The Currency of Fame*, 189.

45. See, for example, the medal by Bombarda of Leonora Cambi (British Museum, London; 1911.6.9.2) reproduced in Scher, *The Currency of Fame*, 190, no. 75.

46. Flaten, *Medals and Plaquettes*, 4, no. 46.

47. Ibid., 48, no. 60. In reality, Queen Christina had a bent back, deformed chest, and misshapen shoulders.

48. Ibid., 51, no. 65. "LIVIVS ODESC[alchi].S[anctae].R[omanae] .E[cclesiae].G[onfarnonarius]." is inscribed around the perimeter of the medal, and the name of the artist and date, "HAMERANVS/.1689," on the shoulder truncation.

49. Two French scholars, Eugène Pilot and Émile Molinier, introduced the term "plaquette" into the scholarship of Renaissance sculpture in the late nineteenth century. Renaissance inventories used the Italian word *medaglia* indiscriminately to refer to antique coins, medals, and plaquettes. Marika Leino, *Fashion, Devotion, and Contemplation: The Status and Functions of Italian Renaissance Plaquettes* (Bern: Peter Lang, 2013), 5–6 and 17. On plaquettes, see *Italian Plaquettes*, ed. Alison Luchs (Washington, DC: National Gallery of Art, 1989). In addition to his catalogue of the Morgenroth collection (note 9) and of a private Milanese collection with coauthor Dagmar Stiebral (*Renaissance Medals and Plaquettes* [Florence: Studio per Edizioni Scelte, 1983]), Middeldorf's publications on plaquettes include "Una miscellanea di placchette," in *Scritti di storia dell'arte in onore di Ugo Procacci*, ed. Grazia Dal Poggetto and Paolo Del Poggetto, 2 vols. (Milan: Electa, 1977), 2:326–30; "A lost plaquette by Vittore Gambello," *Burlington Magazine* 118 (1976): 232; "Su alcune placchette tedesche," *Musei ferraresi* 4 (1974): 144–46; "Filarete?," *Mitteilungen des Kunsthistorischen Institutes in Florenz* 17, no. 1 (1973): 75–86; and "Eine Florentiner Plakette," in *Adolph Goldschmidt zu seinem siebenzigsten Geburtstag* (Berlin: Würfel, 1935), 121–22.

50. According to Leino (117–18), most plaquettes after the antique are casts of hard stone engravings or copies of ancient Roman imperial coins; she has identified approximately 150 plaquette designs based on identifiable antique sources, two thirds of which are portraits.

51. Leino (119 and 129) considers only independent, nonfunctional reliefs to be plaquettes. Other scholars are more inclusive. See, for example, John Pope-Hennessy, "The Study of Italian Plaquettes," in *Italian Plaquettes*, 30, who includes small reliefs on Renaissance oil lamps, sword-pommels, book bindings, armor, horse trappings, pendants, and hat badges in the category.

52. Leino (252–53) cites contemporary accounts of two collections incorporating medals and plaquettes — that assembled by Fra Franceschino da Cesena, librarian of the Malatesta Library, in his study in the monastery in Cesena ca. 1489, and the Gonzaga family's collection, located in "il Studio dell'antiquitate" in the ducal palace in Mantua ca. 1540–42.

53. Leino (17 and 19) notes, "the exact circumstances surrounding the origins of such manufacture [of the first plaquettes] are not clear." She hypothesizes (22) that the earliest plaquettes were made as copies of antique gems in the collections of Pietro Barbo and Lorenzo de' Medici for collectors who could not afford the originals or who did not have access to them.

54. The format of these plaquettes may have been inspired by the example of low-relief roundels on antique oil lamps and pocket mirrors. Douglas Lewis, "The Past and Future of the Italian Plaquette," in *Italian Plaquettes*, 12.

55. Flaten, *Medals and Plaquettes*, 191, no. 318.

56. Pietro Cannata, "Le placchette del Filarete," in *Italian Plaquettes*, 35–53.

57. For a review of previous scholarship regarding the origins of plaquettes with religious subject matter, see Leino (17–18). Leino contends that reproductive plaquettes after the antique preceded the development of plaquettes with religious subjects and that the two types may have evolved independently. Among surviving plaquettes, only around 25 percent have religious subjects, according to Leino (161).

58. Flaten, *Medals and Plaquettes*, 191, no. 319.

59. See Christopher B. Fulton, "The Master I O. F. F. and the Function of Plaquettes," in *Italian Plaquettes*, 143–62.

60. Flaten, *Medals and Plaquettes*, 192, nos. 320 and 321. The second medal, a very rubbed aftercast, represents Cacus stealing the cattle of Hercules.

61. Ibid., 194, no. 323.

62. Ibid., 196, no. 326.

63. Ibid., 196, no. 327.

64. Ibid., 195, no. 324. Leino (95 and 164) notes that Jerome was the saint most often represented on plaquettes.

65. Flaten, *Medals and Plaquettes*, 197, no. 329.

66. Ulrich Middeldorf, review of *Le placchette italiane*, 151–56.

67. Carole Collier Frick, *Dressing Renaissance Florence: Families, Fortunes, and Fine Clothing* (Baltimore: Johns Hopkins University Press, 2002), 96.

68. See Luca Molà, *The Silk Industry in Renaissance Venice* (Baltimore: Johns Hopkins University Press, 2000), xx.

69. Frick, 94: "In practical Florence, because cloth was so excruciatingly essential for rituals demanding public display of familial honor, expensive garments seemed to have been valued by the head of the family only in the context of a specific social and political agenda (marriage alliance, political office, funeral display). When this occasion was accomplished, Florentines cashed in their clothes." Patricia Allerston, "Reconstructing the Second-Hand Clothes Trade in Sixteenth- and Seventeenth-Century Venice," *Costume: The Journal of the Costume Society* 33 (1999): 51–52, cites the example of the Venetian doge Andrea Gritti, who gave his gold-and-white ducal mantle and matching gown to the Venetian monastery of San Francesco della Vigna, to be made into wall hangings for the church.

70. In cases where the gilt and silvered threads have survived intact, the metal is more often than not abraded or, in the case of silver, discolored due to oxidation.

71. Jacqueline Herald, *Renaissance Dress in Italy, 1400–1500* (London: Bell & Hyman, 1981), 86; and Lisa Monnas, *Merchants, Princes and Painters: Silk Fabrics in Italian and Northern Paintings, 1300–1500* (New Haven, CT: Yale University Press, 2009), 16.

72. All three were woven with first-grade silk, i.e., silk thread made by carefully unwinding the intact cocoon in a basin of hot water to form one long, continuous thread. Italy — principally the regions of Tuscany and mainland Venice — produced the raw materials, but it was necessary to import silk from Spain and elsewhere to meet the demands of production.

73. The ground may consist of: 1) plain or tabby weave, the most basic weave, in which the weft passes over and under every other warp thread; 2) twill weave, in which the weft floats over and under a specified number of warp threads in each row but shifts over one pace in each subsequent row, thereby creating a pattern of diagonal parallel ribs; 3) or a combination of plain and twill weaves.

74. The type of metal thread changed over time. In the fourteenth century, the thread (*filé*) was made of gilt strips of animal-gut membrane wrapped around a line core. In the fifteenth century, the thread consisted of a silver-gilt strip wrapped around a silk core. As of the late fifteenth century, a drawn

wire thread was often used. Monnas, *Princes and Painters*, 299–300; and idem, *Renaissance Velvets* (London: V & A Publishing, 2012), 19–20.

75. On Renaissance velvets, see Monnas, *Renaissance Velvets*.

76. The adjective *inferriata*, meaning "grill" or "grating," refers to the fact that the curvilinear patterns of this type of voided velvet reflect the ornate ironwork of the period. Two early examples of *ferronerie* textile design are in the Middeldorf Collection (IUAM acc. nos. 91.99 [fig. 33] and 91.106.1/2).

77. Regarding these so-called cloths of gold, see Monnas, *Princes and Painters*, 299–300.

78. Frick (95 and 98) records that fabrics produced in fifteenth-century Florence cost from almost 3 florins per braccio for fine wool up to 20 florins per braccio for velvet brocades with gold or silver threads; damasks ran from $3\frac{1}{2}$ florins to 1 florin per braccio. To put this cost into perspective, Frick notes that a family of four living in Renaissance Florence between the years 1440 and 1480 could live at a basic level on 56 to 70 florins annually.

79. Red was produced with plant madder or kermes (insect) dyes. Herald, 90–92; and Frick, 101–3.

80. For similar textiles, see Rosalia Bonito Fanelli, *Five Centuries of Italian Textiles, 1300–1800* (Prato: Museo del Tessuto, 1981), 88–89.

81. Both the hood and the cope have the inscription "ASSVNTA EST" woven into the textile. The phrase is derived from "Assumpta est Maria in caelum, gaudent angeli" ("Mary has been taken up into heaven; the angels rejoice"), a devotional text that is part of the liturgy of the Feast of the Assumption.

82. For comparable textiles, see Fanelli, 92–93. Among the textile producers in Italy, the weavers of Perugia were also known for specialty woven fabrics. The Middeldorf Collection includes a number of Perugian woven linen towels and tablecloths with decorative borders.

83. The color of textiles depended upon the type and quality of the dyes, the mordant (the substance used to set the dye), and the length of time the fibers were dyed. Dyestuffs constituted a major cost in the production of textiles. On dyeing, see Molà, 107–21.

84. This type of embroidery is also known as *lacis* or *filet brodé*.

85. Cole, x.

CHECKLIST OF THE EXHIBITION

All works collection of Indiana University Art Museum unless otherwise noted.

MEDALS

Fifteenth Century

87.26.2.53   Florence, ca. 1440; Pope Eugenius IV and the Council of
              Florence, 1439: Pope Eugenius IV enthroned (obv.); Saint
              Peter and Emperor John VIII Palaiologos kneeling (rev.).
              Bronze; aftercast; 51 millimeters.

87.26.2.127   Florence, ca. 1470s; Cosimo de' Medici: Bust of Cosimo
              (obv.); Personification of Florence (rev.) Silver; struck
              (or cast of struck original); 37 millimeters.

87.26.2.51   Matteo de' Pasti (active 1441–1467/68); Sigismundo Pandolfo
              Malatesta, 1446: Bust of Sigismundo Malatesta (obv.);
              Casque with coronet on a tilted shield, elephant head crest
              and manteling (rev.). Bronze; aftercast; 41 millimeters.

87.26.2.52   Rome; Pope Paul II, 1465: Bust of Paul II (obv.);
              Palazzo Venezia (rev.) Bronze; cast; 33 millimeters; Rome.

87.26.2.47   Giovanni Candida (Giovanni di Salvatore Filangieri;
              ca. 1445/50–1498/99?); Maximilian I and Mary of Burgundy,
              ca. 1477–78: Bust of Maximilian I (obv.); Mary of Burgundy
              (rev.). Bronze; cast; 48 millimeters.

Sixteenth Century

87.26.2.65   Domenico de' Vetri (after 1480–ca. 1547); Duke Cosimo I
              de' Medici, ca. 1540: Bust of Cosimo I (obv.); Capricorn, eight
              stars (rev.) Bronze; struck; 35 millimeters.

87.26.2.59   Domenico de' Vetri; Duke Cosimo I de' Medici, ca. 1540:
              Bust of Cosimo I (obv.); Hygeia, goddess of health,
              with a staff and bowl (rev.). Bronze; struck; 35 millimeters.

87.26.2.60	Pastorino de Pastorini (ca.1508–1592); Ludovico Ariosto: Bust of Ariosto (obv.); Bees pouring forth from a hive on fire (rev.). Bronze; cast; 37 millimeters.
87.26.2.62	Domenico Poggini (1520–1590) and Gianpaolo Poggini (1518–1582); Princess Eleonora of Toledo, ca. 1551: Bust of Eleonora of Toledo (obv.); Peahen with wings spread sheltering six chicks (rev.). Bronze; cast; 44 millimeters.
87.26.2.71	Domenico Poggini (1520–1590) and Gianpaolo Poggini (1518–1582); Duke Francesco I de' Medici and Archduchess Joanna of Austria, 1565: Bust of Francesco I (obv.); Bust of Joanna of Austria (rev.). Bronze; struck; 40 millimeters.
87.26.2.58	Pier Paolo Galeotti, called Romano (1520–1584); Duke Cosimo I de' Medici, ca. 1561: Bust of Cosimo I (obv.); View of the Uffizi and Palazzo Vecchio with statue of Justice (rev.). Bronze; struck; 41 millimeters.
87.26.2.46	Paolo Galeotti, called Romano (1520–1584); Grand Duke Cosimo I de' Medici, 1569: Bust of Cosimo I (obv.); Medici shield of arms surmounted by the grand ducal crown (rev.). Silver; struck; 44 millimeters.
87.26.2.54	Giovanni dal Cavino (1500–1570); Emperor Septimius Severus, mid-16th century: Bust of Septimius Severus (obv.); Mars nude holding spear and shield and cuirass by his side (rev.). Bronze; cast from a struck original; 39 millimeters.
87.26.2.56	Giovanni dal Cavino (1500–1570); Empress Annia Galeria Faustina, mid-16th-century: Bust of Empress Faustina (obv.); Six figures sacrificing around an altar (rev.). Bronze; cast from a struck original; 36 millimeters.
87.26.2.45	Giovanni dal Cavino (1500–1570); Giovanni Melsi, 1560s: Bust of Melsi (obv.); Melsi as Genius (rev.). Bronze; struck; 36 millimeters.
87.26.2.49	Leone Leoni (ca. 1509–1590); Jupiter Thundering Against the Giants, 1549: Jupiter throwing lightning bolts at a multitude of giants (obv.); empty reverse. Bronze; cast; 73 millimeters.
87.26.2.61	Agostino and Alessandro Ardenti (active, second half of the

16th century); Pietro Macchiavelli, late 16th century: Bust of Macchiavelli (obv.); empty reverse. Silver with traces of gilding; cast; 84 millimeters.

87.26.2.72   Bombarda (Giovanni Battista Cambi?, active 1540–1582?); Violenta Brasavola Pigna (Nicolucci), third quarter of the 16th century: Bust of Violenta Brasavola (obv.); empty reverse. Lead; cast; 71 millimeters.

Seventeenth Century

87.26.2.93   Gaspare Mola (ca. 1580–1640); Grand Duke Ferdinand I de' Medici, 1608: Bust of Ferdinand I (obv.); empty rev. Bronze; cast; 90 millimeters.

87.26.2.89   Gaspare Mola (ca. 1580–1640); Grand Duke Cosimo II de' Medici, 1618: Bust of Cosimo II (obv.); scepter and coronet surrounded by the Medici balls (rev.). Bronze; struck; 39 millimeters.

87.26.2.79   Gaspare Morone-Mola (active 1627–1669); Pope Alexander VII, 1657: Bust of Alexander VII (obv.); bird's-eye view of Saint Peter's and colonnade (rev.). Gilded bronze; cast; 72 millimeters.

87.26.2.94   Gaspare Morone-Mola (active 1627–1669); Grand Duke Cosimo III de' Medici, 1666: Bust of Cosimo III (obv.); Ship on sea with four stars and blazon in the sky (rev.). Bronze; struck; 49 millimeters.

87.26.2.101   Giovanni Battista Gugliemada (?) (active 1665–1689); Queen Christina of Sweden, 1680s: Bust of Queen Christina (obv.); Lion with eleven stars, a rudder, globe, and cornucopia (rev.). Bronze; cast from a struck original (?); 62 millimeters.

87.26.2.95   Giovanni Martino Hamerani (1646–1705); Prince Livio Odescalchi, 1689: Bust of Livio Odescalchi (obv.); Radiant sun rising over Eastern Europe (rev.). Bronze; struck; 62 millimeters.

87.26.2.111   Massimiliano Soldani Benzi (1656–1740); Francesco Redi, 1684; Bust of Redi (obv.); Minerva with lance, revealing Nature with a serpent and stag (rev.). Silver; cast; 87 millimeters.

PLAQUETTES

87.26.2.8	Italy; 15th century; after the antique; Hermaphroditus with three putti; gilded bronze; cast; 30 x 35 millimeters.
87.26.2.7	Master I O. F. F. (Giovanni Fonduli; ca. 1430–ca. 1497); Judgment of Paris; gilded bronze; probably modern aftercast; 56 millimeters.
87.26.2.9	Master I O. F. F. (Giovanni Fonduli; ca. 1430–ca. 1497); Hercules and Nemean Lion; gilded bronze; modern aftercast; 51 millimeters.
72.45	Ulocrino (active ca. 1485); The Death of Meleager; bronze; cast; 73 x 54 millimeters.
87.26.2.10	Venice; early 16th century; Saint Jerome in Penitence; bronze; cast; 92 x 68 millimeters.
87.26.2.4	Valerio Belli (ca. 1468–1546); Fortune; lead; struck; 37 x 29 millimeters.
87.26.2.5	After Valerio Belli; Diana; lead; struck; 35 x 28 millimeters.
87.26.2.2	Venice; late 16th century; Trinity; bronze; cast; 94 x 79 millimeters.

TEXTILES

87.26.1.673	Fragment. Silk. Cut voided velvet on satin weave ground. 63.5 x 33.34 centimeters. Italy, mid-15th century.
91.108.1–2	Fragments of a chasuble. Silk. Cut voided velvet on satin weave ground. 117.5 x 25.8 centimeters (91.106.1); 118.5 x 27 centimeters (91.106.2). Italy, mid- to late 15th century.
91.99	Panel. Silk and linen. Cut velvet. 186.5 x 58 centimeters. Italy, possibly Florence, late 15th century.
87.26.1.174	Fragment. Silk. Pile-on-pile velvet on plain weave ground. 16 x 14.5 centimeters. Italy, 15th–16th century.
87.26.1.672	Fragment. Silk. Cut and uncut velvet on plain weave ground. 25.5 x 17.5 centimeters. Italy, 15th–16th century.
87.26.1.4	Fragment. Silk and silver strips. Cut and uncut velvet on plain

weave ground. 25.5 x 17.5 centimeters. Italy, second half of the 16th century.

87.26.1.220b	Fragment. Silk. Cut and uncut velvet. 47.5 x 7.5 centimeters. Italy or Spain, 16th century.
87.26.1.201	Fragment. Silk. Cut and uncut velvet. 53.2 x 25.4 centimeters. Italy or Spain, 16th–17th century.
87.26.1.1122	Annunciation. Rectangular panel (apparel?). Silk, linen, and silver metal threads. Lampas. Brocatelle. 37.8 x 34.8 centimeters. Italy, probably Tuscany, second half of the 15th century.
91.143	Man of Sorrows. Orphrey band. Silk and linen. Lampas. Brocatelle. 114 x 21.8 centimeters. Italy, probably Tuscany, second half of the 15th century.
91.148	Virgin Giving Her Girdle to Saint Thomas. Orphrey band. Silk, linen, and silver metal threads. Lampas. Brocatelle. 118.5 x 23.5 centimeters. Italy, probably Tuscany, second half of the 15th century.
91.150	Virgin Giving Her Girdle to Saint Thomas. Hood of a cope (companion to 91.148). Silk, linen, and silver metal threads. Lampas. Brocatelle. 40 x 42 centimeters. Italy, probably Tuscany, second half of the 15th century.
87.26.1.803	Fragment. Silk. Damask. Plain and twill weave. 44.5 x 32.2 centimeters. Italy, 16th century.
87.26.1.282	Fragment. Silk. Lampas. Plain weave. 26.3 x 26.5 centimeters. Italy, 16th–17th century.
87.26.1.340A	Fragment. Moired silk. Brocading tied in plain and twill weave. 33.3 x 17.4 centimeters. Italy, 16th–17th century.
87.26.1.905	Chasuble fragment (?). Silk and linen. Lampas. Brocatelle. 45 x 50 centimeters. Spain or Italy, 16th–17th century.
87.26.1.1113	Chasuble fragment (?). Silk and linen. Lampas. Brocatelle. 49 x 26.8 centimeters. Spain, 16th–17th century.
87.26.1.1114	Fragment. Silk and linen. Lampas. Brocatelle. 37.5 x 22.5 centimeters. Spain, 16th–17th century.
87.26.1.924	Fragment. Silk and linen. Lampas. Brocatelle. 24 x 47.5 centimeters. Spain, 16th–17th century.

87.26.1.935   Panel. Silk and linen. Lampas. Brocatelle.
45.5 x 37 centimeters. Spain, 16th–17th century.

87.26.1.943   Fragment. Silk and linen. Lampas. Brocatelle.
40.16 x 47.94 centimeters. Spain, 16th–17th century.

87.26.1.127   Fragment. Silk. Lampas. Plain weave.
19 x 10.5 centimeters. Italy, 17th century.

87.26.1.668   Fragment. Silk and gilt metal strips. Brocading tied in
satin weave. 47.5 x 20.5 centimeters. Italy, 17th century.

87.26.1.132   Fragment. Silk and gilt metal threads. Satin weave.
25.2 x 24.8 centimeters. Italy, 17th century.

87.26.1.53   Fragment. Wool and linen. Double cloth.
50.5 x 10.5 centimeters. Italy, 17th century.

87.26.1.56   Fragment. Wool and linen. Double cloth.
21 x 22.5 centimeters. Italy, 17th century.

87.26.1.57   Fragment. Wool and linen. Double cloth.
26 x 15 centimeters. Italy, 17th century.

87.26.1.58   Fragment. Wool. Double cloth.
13.49 x 13.01 centimeters. Italy, 17th century.

87.26.1.60   Fragment. Wool and linen. Double cloth.
51 x 11 centimeters. Italy, 17th century.

87.26.1.689   Section of a border. Silk and gilt and silver metal threads.
Needlework. Darned netting. 67.8 x 13 centimeters.
Italy, 16th century.

87.26.1.763   Section of a border. Linen and red silk thread. Plain weave
with needlework. Embroidery and darned netting.
33 x 16 centimeters. Italy, 17th century.

87.26.1.764   Cushion. Linen and red silk thread. Plain weave with
needlework. Embroidery. 48 x 40 centimeters, including
toggles. England or Italy, early 17th century.
Dalmatic, Anonymous, Italian, ca. 1450–75. Orphreys,
embroidery, silk and metallic thread on linen plain weave,
velvet. 104.1 x 111.8 centimeters. Detroit Institute of Arts,
Gift of Mr. and Mrs. Edgar B. Whitcomb. Acc. no. 37.56.